D0848196

MOVING MATTERS

MOVING MATTERS

Paths of Serial Migration

Susan Ossman

Stanford University Press
Stanford, California

Printed in the United States of America on acid-free, archival-quality paper

Library of Congress Cataloging-in-Publication Data

Ossman, Susan, author.
 Moving matters : paths of serial migration / Susan Ossman.
     pages   cm.
 Includes bibliographical references and index.
 ISBN 978-0-8047-7028-6 (cloth : alk. paper) —
 ISBN 978-0-8047-7029-3 (pbk. : alk. paper)
  1. Emigration and immigration—Social aspects. 2. Emigration and
immigration—Psychological aspects. 3. Immigrants—Social life and customs.
4. Cosmopolitanism. I. Title.

JV6225O77 2013
304.8—dc23

                                                            2012033971

Typeset at Stanford University Press in 10.5/15 Adobe Garamond

#809365700

For those who are forced to move
and those held in place against their will.

CONTENTS

ACKNOWLEDGMENTS

Grants from the John Simon Guggenheim Foundation and the British Academy made this book possible. The hospitality of Fatima Badry Zalami, Alexandru Balesescu, Kathleen Chevalier, Jean-Noël Ferrié and Souad Radi, Nabiha Jerad, Bayan Kanoo, Shannon McNulty, Susan Perry, Hassan and Rachida Rachik and the Ouadahi family made it utterly pleasurable. Their generosity often extended to identifying potential interviewees and traveling with me to distant cities. I am especially grateful to Leila Abouhouraira and Jamal Ouadahi for follow-up interviews in Quebec and to Yasmine Ouadahi for transcribing them. Elizabeth Shlala recorded four life histories in London. Leila, Jamal and Elizabeth make appearances in the coming pages. Other friends do not. Yet, each of them, like the dozens of serial migrants I met in the course of research contributed to the general description I propose.

The idea of serial migration was sparked in a conversation with Todd Gitlin. The concept took form through conversations with Susan Terrio while I was teaching at Georgetown University from 2001 to 2004. Elzbieta Gozdziak encouraged me to write about it and

Michael Maas' help with grant proposals was invaluable. Chris Berry took over my classes so I could travel while I was on the faculty at Goldsmith's College, where from 2005 to 2007 I was lucky to enjoy the lively atmosphere of the media and communications department. Amina Aouchar, Doug Barnert, Marie-Agnes Beau, James Curran, Shana Cohen, Nick Couldry, Rupert Cox, Daniel Dayan, Waddick Doyle, Evelyn Early, Stephen Foster, John Ganem, Dierdre Gilfedder, Abderrahmane Lakhsassi, Wessie Ling, Justin MacGuinness, Nick Mai, Ruth Mandel, Noha Mellor, Dave Morley, Alice Peinado, Caroline Pierce, Elitza Ranova, Arnd Schneider, Julie Thomas and Adeline Wrona offered stimulating ideas on this research. George Marcus has encouraged many anthropologists to strike out in new directions or think things through differently; since I moved to Southern California in 2007 I have been happy to enjoy his company and ideas about ethnographic design more often. In Riverside, Anne Sutherland, Charles Louis, the Warrens, Phyllis Lovell, Paul Velen and the neighbors on Isabella Street made this serial migrant feel welcome. At UCR Christina Schwenkel and Paul Ryer have become especially precious interlocutors on anthropology, migration and life. In difficult times the Global Studies committee has kept my spirits up; I especially thank Juliann Allison, Chris Chase-Dunn, Anil Deolalikar, Bronwyn Leebow and Perry Link for their confidence and enthusiasm. Sharon Payne, Brenda Aragon, Victoria Cross and Brandy Quarles-Clark have kept things moving smoothly in the office.

Kate Wahl of Stanford University Press has been unwavering in her support throughout the long writing process. Katya Rice's comprehensive editing assistance and sensitive attention to detail was phenomenal. Gareth Stanton and an anonymous reader generously offered well deserved criticisms of the original manuscript along with encouragement. I hope that they will find the book improved owing to their suggestions. Mark Kuroczko's insistence on poetics has been an inspiration for more years than I care to count. In spite of his aversion to travel James Faubion understood exactly what this book was about from the start. He and WR Duell make life better. So does Ann Henstrand, who has made her homes joyful meeting places for so many years. My parents, Camille and Edward Ossman, have moved about but always been there. As a child my son, Nathanael Dorent, had little choice but to follow my migratory path. Now, I travel to Timbuktu or London or Paris to visit his building projects and exhibitions. Gratitude is too frivolous a word to describe my debt to those who have known me for so long. Or to Rogers Brubaker, who invited me to a place he called primordial and led me to reimagine what *fixations de bonheur* might involve. I do thank him for keeping me on the path to completion.

MOVING MATTERS

INTRODUCTION

Writers, scholars, and media pundits have of late been preoccupied with the way in which movement makes our world. Researchers duly chart the direction of flows of capital and goods; governments take into account the reach of global media in shaping political platforms and cultural policies. Yet, in our haste to trace the trajectories of goods, people, or ways of life we may fail to perceive that a specific pattern of mobility may be as critical as culture, language, or national origin in shaping individual subjects and ways of life. At a time when politics might be best studied as a strategic choreography, the production of politically relevant social difference is obviously related to who moves where when. Yet our understanding of how specific experiences of mobility and settlement might lead people whose paths never cross to envision their lives in a similar manner is hazy. We tend to describe different kinds of travelers, figures like the cosmopolitan, the nomad, or the immigrant, rather than attending to specific migratory trails.[1]

In this essay in ethnography, I try to understand how ways of moving produce forms of life by following people who like myself have immigrated once, then moved again to a third homeland. I consider how the path we have taken has made us serial migrants regardless of our origins or destinations.[2]

To explore how a story of successive dwelling in different countries leads to a form of life is a radical departure from conventional ways of thinking about what makes people alike and why they migrate. Studying people on the move as Chinese or Lebanese, Jewish or Sikh enables researchers and activists to sketch out a space of social or cultural continuity as context. However, to give primacy to ethnicity or culture *a priori* makes it difficult to evaluate the actual importance of these elements. Similarly, in spite of increasing research illustrating the complexity of subjective motivations there is a tendency to assume that most are displaced by the push and pull of market forces. Ethnicity and race, class and cultural dispositions figure in the stories of serial migrants. By first examining how a shared pattern of settlement leads people to use borders to punctuate their life stories and then contemplating how this makes them different from others, the nature of these modes of identification and association becomes clearer.

In working through this object of study that is also the story of my life, it could appear that I fashion myself a native in order to create a people in her own image or imagine myself a prospective ethnographer of a would-be collective that does not even exist in the minds of those who compose it. I make no claim to study any community, however, just as I do not focus on how those I follow might act as agents of change in their adopted homelands, their very foreignness a source of creativity.[3] The point of this research is neither to form a group nor to understand the possible impact of the serial migrant on settled societies but to explore how particular patterns of movement shape ways of dwelling that signal emerging forms of social and cultural organization more generally.[4]

Anthropologists have always been concerned with little recognized ways of life and invisible powers that shape social worlds. Serial migrants are identified by their passages across the most blatant of borders and most basic maps: they cannot be studied "in context." But are ethnographic truths not discovered by plunging into the waters of shared experience? Isn't the anthropologist's legitimacy derived from long familiarity with particular peoples and places and environments? Setting out from my own moves among three continents to follow others to places where I will never set foot and states now erased from the world map by the march of history might seem a sure way to dissolve the scholarly legitimacy of my research. If being there is everything, how might one imagine ethnographic research without a setting? How might one study a way of life that is not passed down through unconscious gestures or traditional practices or beliefs but rather produced by successive displacements across limits set by the crudest maps of international politics?

James Faubion has pointed out that "the ethnographer is able to engage in self-monitoring, a cross-checking, that methodologically more pure research may not allow," and that ethnography is "a pathetic method and its 'pathology' engages (and changes) the fieldworker's mindful body not merely analytically but intuitively, affectively; it is a way at once of being and feeling (the) human."[5] As I encountered serial migrants, followed their paths (pathologies?), and recorded their stories, I sensed a common irritation at being served up remedies for problems reputed to accompany migration. One symptom of our most characteristic infirmities is the restless searching for a narrative form that would join our stories to a collective history. This problem cannot be treated with potions for motion sickness measured in doses of adaptation and integration or medicines concocted to cure immigrants of the pain of uprooting or fitting into their second homeland. Such "remedies" only make matters worse because they obscure the specifics of our journeys. The immigrant is perpetually caught between two places; he is defined by a life in between. But a second migration leads beyond the duality of the immigrant's situation. It introduces a serial logic into the life story, opening a horizon of further displacement.[6] Serial migrants' narratives indicate that they generally feel settling in a third country as a liberation from the double bind of immigration. However, they find it hard to articulate this experience in positive terms because what for them is an essential transformation goes largely unrecognized. Border crossings generate the serial migrant as a specific kind of subject, whatever her content. Yet the efforts she makes to bring her features into focus and establish a coherent line of action can require apparent inconsistencies of expression in the present.

Repeated migration includes the possibility of joining different ways of life, systems of belief, and politics, but it also raises questions: Who am I, in addition to, or in spite of, these differences? One must try to sort out the self amid these collections while becoming increasingly suspicious of how borders are drawn among cultures, political systems, or ethical perspectives. How might one conceive of oneself as a coherent subject when so many forms of self-identification might be so variously linked to practices of day-to-day life? How might one tell one's story in several languages and recognize one's own face according to coexisting principles of vision? Disparities among an individual's diverse social roles have long been the subject of social inquiry, not to mention the stuff from which novels and plays are born. The experience of migration often accentuates discrepancies of how or when or for whom one performs apparently similar roles. The serial migrant is not simply many things to many people; he is shaped by the variations among the systematic ways he is construed in the places of his experience. Some of these systems correspond to divisions between states; others do not. But the way in which modes of identification and rules of performance tend to be associated with particular political, cultural, or linguistic environments could suggest that the serial migrant is a rich collective of remnants of the wholes that make up ordinary social life. His life may appear as a creative amalgam of found objects or a *bricolage* of diverse cultural materials, but this does not solve the problem of developing a continuous self. The serial migrant's difficulty with difference is thus not simply that of being "other"; her problem with diversity is internal.[7] The eternal addition of hyphenated identities is the question for her, not an answer. It is not a distance from origins and others but a potential for over-involvement with places and people that characterizes the serial migrant's dilemma. She suffers from over-definition.[8]

The value of motion assumed by this peripatetic form of settlement has little in common with the idea that a boundary-crossing life offers an escape from habits ensconced in inherited social reflexes or traditions. Nor does it jibe with the striving for increased status or income or cultural capital that is often assumed to establish a parallel between physical and social mobility. Instead, it dwells on the possibilities for self-definition presented by confronting the multiplicity of the self in ways that are peculiarly objectified.[9] The self is made neither as a unique expression of an original culture nor as some heady brew of mixed traditions, but in a process of ongoing consideration of what links the places of one's life (besides oneself) as well as how different institutions and histories distinguish them. Serial migrants' movements may seem unhindered, their lives a symbol of postmodern fluidity, but they are defined by borders at their most fundamental. Borders of belief, language, or cultural practice often fail to follow state lines, but for the serial migrant political boundaries fixed on maps are vital markers of her life.

COMMON DREAMS

No one is born a serial migrant, and anyone might become one. Where might one go to meet people who never congregate, speak no single language, and belong to no particular organization, subjects who can be identified only once one knows something about their story? The common ground of serial migration cannot be visited. Intriguingly, however, many of the serial migrants I spoke with reported having had essentially the same dream, one in which all of their friends and relations were brought together, just once, in a single place and time. Waking or sleeping, they imagined family and friends coming together for some grand occasion, a voyage or a feast at which they spoke one another's languages. I often have these dreams myself; one was especially vivid, for it was silent. Instead of listening to my mother speak Arabic or my sister speak French, I watched as words flowed soundlessly from the lips of a friend on tiny pieces of paper traced in different scripts.

In the spirit of gathering people together to speak in tongues, I decided that before trying to follow serial migrants I might instead invite some of them to come together. I convened a meeting in 2004 at Georgetown University, limiting participation to those who shared a single homeland, either as a point of origin or as one of their lands of settlement.[10] I chose Morocco as this common framework; it was my third homeland, so I knew many other people who had passed through the kingdom.[11] One might have imagined such a seminar leading to exchanges of our different perspectives on Morocco from the point of view of our various origins or native cultures, citizenships, or the historical moment when we each lived in Marrakech or Casablanca. Might we have found evidence of some inchoate national sentiment shared by native-born and immigrant? But instead our conversations focused on the way the country we shared took on meaning in relation to our life stories. It was the process by which each of our homelands was situated in our life narratives that came to dominate our conversations and the texts we later published.[12]

Those who met in 2004 focused on their modes of settlement rather than extolling their mobility. They expressed discomfort at equations of themselves with most images of the cosmopolitan, and spoke of "immigration" as an experience they had passed through instead of a personal or social problem to be solved. These concerns shaped the diagnostics of the next step of study. As I moved beyond the framework of any specific territory and tried to imagine where serial migrants might tend to settle, if only for a time, I determined to seek out serial migrants in locations where there are many migrants and where there is a high rate of turnover of the population. Washington DC, London, Manama, Paris, Cairo, Doha, Dubai, Montreal, and New York were some of the places where I recorded life stories and carried out fieldwork.[13] My encounters were enabled by the history of my own displacements: I relied on friends and acquaintances I had known for decades whose lives had led them to move across international borders on several occasions.

In the manner of the serial migrant I am, when faced with an accumulation of habits collected here and there, of objects to be kept or discarded in preparation for an impending move, I have had to move forward not with a full collection of available ideas or texts, or even fully utilizing those I have read, but with a privileging of certain ways of asking questions I developed in the course of living in France, Morocco, England, and the United States, working in Belgium and Tunisia, and staying for extended periods in Cairo, Montreal, and the Arab principalities of the Persian Gulf. In developing this research I chose to focus on those who had moved of their own volition rather than in the tow of global corporations, missionary networks, or diplomatic corps.[14] Similarly, in my interviews I did not include household servants who travel the world following one employer. Those who move in the context of jobs with a single employer or as workers in international agencies share some experiences with those I followed. But those who follow their jobs have less at stake than those who move without the protection of a continuous organizational or social milieu, which enables them to maintain a stable measure of their career, for instance. Some of those whose stories I tell in the following pages grew up in diplomatic households, were military brats, or followed a parent's job from place to place, but they appear here because of the direction they took once they were adults. A few of the individuals

I introduce took on huge responsibilities before they reached legal adulthood: some as child migrants or refugees, others as the children of refugees and immigrants who helped their parents learn to cope in their new country. I include those experiences in their stories, but I did not seek out minors who are at present in such circumstances. Although I recount household interactions I witnessed and was part of, the youngest person I interviewed individually was twenty-two, the eldest seventy-three. A certain number of years had to elapse before the story of a serial migrant could unfold. It was through these individual stories that I came to explore the way the family or groups of friends might become entangled to form a collective migratory subject. Two of the people you will meet in this book chose to be represented by a pseudonym. I elected to add three more to this list given the evolution of migration policies since these meetings. For most I use their real first names as they requested when they were interviewed.[15]

IDENTIFICATIONS

To search for serial migrants was to elicit commentary on the object of research. When I inquired about possible interviewees, some found it presumptuous of me to carry out a study of people who formed no group with recognizable traits. Others suggested that the lifestyle of serial migrants was made possible by their wealth, education, and cosmopolitan outlook. Shouldn't poor refugees or exiles be the object of my study? While some in the audiences who listened to me explain this work imagined my project as focused on footloose elites, others recognized figures of the refugee, the exile, or the migrant worker pushed to move to a third nation by an inhospitable regime, violent militia, or market forces as its potential protagonists. In our unjust and unequal world, some people wondered how I could fail to define the object of research in terms of the intersection of nationality, ethnicity, gender, and class. To some my approach seemed to ignore the importance of cultural bonds. For others, to focus on the path rather than the function of the migratory subject as a cog in the machine of the neo-liberal economy was a political *faux pas*. Others were unabashedly enthusiastic about this research, but their excitement was often the result of a misunderstanding. Several encouraged me to revise the definition of serial migrants to include them in my sample; hadn't they traveled widely or spent a "year abroad"?[16] Why not include those who were fluent in several languages? These interlocutors tended to assume that I was trying to study the value of "international experience" for developing a critical distance, the kind of intellectual *dépaysement* that is in fact classically associated with travel as well as anthropological field methods, and more recently revived in discussions about cosmopolitanism.

Some colleagues urged me to admit that I was really working out a specific angle on the "cosmopolitan perspective."[17] Others thought I would gain more from comparing serial migrants to nomads: perhaps these serial migrants were avatars of a drifting population of a future time when roots and origins would be severed for everyone. In the first two chapters, I do my best to take their suggestions. It would, however, require a book—or two or several—to enumerate the debates currently circling around the cosmopolitan and the nomad. The features of each are so general that to define them fully would be to engage in a polemic that would lead me off the path I seek to follow. Instead, I draw up portraits of both, then use them as backgrounds against which to project stories of serial migrants, leading me to suggest that they are complementary and that each is too broadly construed to explain how movement makes subjects through particular forms of experience.

Cosmopolitans take shape in a flight away from or across some settled place, whether it is conceived as a culture, a nation, an opinion, or a state's hold on its territory. This conceptual move gives rise to an expectation that modes of subjectivity might be altered, new forms of politics devised as a result of a critical departure from taken-for-granted habits and modes of thought. Some link the process of critical self-reflection to the experience of learning of other ways of life through travel and migration. This type of person, however, is defined not by a particular pattern of physical mobility but by a peculiarly detached relationship to places and, one would imagine, other people. Everywhere, the cosmopolitan inhabits a space of distanced deliberation and comparison. Even while remaining a patriot, the measure of her politics is the world at large. In contrast, the serial migrant tends not to envision a cosmopolitics that arises from the move away from the earth, from the local to the global or the planetary. This particular form of mobile experience actually produces an increased awareness of frontiers and limits, whether these are political, linguistic, or religious.

In contrast to the cosmopolitan, who seems tolerant and open and willing to go everywhere, remote as she is from taken-for-granted cultural and social ties, the serial migrant uses ordinary maps and common cultural labels to strategically work on himself by submitting himself to different social and political arrangements. Although a few of the serial migrants I met tried very hard to develop something like a "cosmopolitan perspective" in order to compare the places of their lives with equanimity, most firmly rejected the idea that they might be perceived as exemplars of this worldly figure because it was too abstract, too intellectual, and often too self-conscious in its pretension to take part in global political discussions.

Nomads and wanderers may appear romantic because, like business travelers or the very rich, they manage to take their habits along with them wherever they travel. Indeed, those who can do this with minimal means signal most clearly that their wanderlust arises from some purely internal, intrinsic motivation. Their ease of displacement appears to be a sign of some authentic internal value. Might one turn to Deleuze and Guattari's elaboration of the figure of the nomad to develop a more embodied, more practically oriented, less discursive understanding of mobile lives? I entertain this possibility in the second chapter but quickly run into problems assimilating the serial migrant to this peripatetic figure, portrayed by the philosophers as moving so smoothly that he does not even register the existence of the borders he crosses. Serial migrants may dream of such a graceful dance across the earth, but ultimately borders are what defines them. Indeed, one might say they repeatedly seek them out in a process of self-definition. Unlike the nomad, they are generally willing to submit themselves to the most various ways of being identified by government agencies and their neighbors. To see in them an incarnation of the celebrated concept of the nomad is to ignore how repeated settlement shapes them. Yet, to focus on their settlement rather than their motion leads to another way of misrecognizing their experience. Once they are perceived from this angle, they appear simply as people from somewhere else; they are classified as immigrants.

In contrast to the cosmopolitan, whose motion is from the particular to the general, and to the nomad, who may travel unhindered across landscapes unmarked by borders, the immigrant always moves from one place to another. His life unfolds between two countries. To be of two nations, configured by two political systems and confused by speaking two languages, makes him a figure characterized by a fundamental cleavage.[18] What happens when someone steps beyond the duality of immigration? Does she enter a hybrid realm of the imagination or entertain a more complex and ambivalent relationship with the immigrant's Janus-faced reality? An embodied being can travel from one place to another only at any given time; to move, then, is to be caught between two locations. Although the doppelgangers of one's market presence, one's multiple identifications by self and others in the clouds of the Internet, and indeed the life one continues to live in places of previous settlement, in the time lag of statistics and postal addresses and in the form of institutions one participated in, the living subject must contend with the limits of the body.[19] While migrating to a third homeland introduces a logically infinite set of places one might move on to, the simple truth is that anybody can settle in only a few places in the course of a lifetime. Each displacement serves as a reminder of those homes where one does not dwell at present.

Setting the serial migrant against the image of the immigrant leads to a more fruitful direction of analysis than does reflection on cosmopolitan ideals or engagement in nomadic modes of action. Most often migration is supposed to be a once-in-a-lifetime ordeal, a rite of passage that enables the migrant to occupy a new status as an immigrant. In the third chapter I suggest that when this rite of passage is reiterated, migration takes on certain ritual aspects. The reiteration of the migration story goes unnoticed, however; there is no public acknowledgment of this repetition or what it entails for the subject. It was only through years of listening to stories of serial migration and being drawn to articulate my own experience that I came to see what a fundamental shift this repetition entailed. The move from a second homeland to a third country introduces an open-ended logic to the immigrant story and leads people to use borders as a way of structuring their life story. I analyze how the experience of repeat migration encourages a particular way of transforming homelands into signposts of the periods of one's life.[20] A path of serial migration leads to a form of life "emplotment."[21] The places, states, societies, or contexts that are assumed to produce peoples and cultures and national feeling, the communities where immigrants appear as foreign bodies, become the material from which to shape a form of life that engages multiplicity not in general, not all at once, but in succession. This leads to specific ways of problematizing the self, the state, and social relationships.

The immigrant may suffer from being perceived as a stranger, but the serial migrant struggles with an accumulation of ways of being "other." He thus points to the limits of the additive logic of hyphenation and the syncretic urges of the hybrid that have inspired a politics of difference made of the building blocks of culture, suggesting new forms of commonality. What serial migrants share is neither a perspective nor an ideology, and certainly not an aversion to settlement, but a way of making themselves of their several homelands by repeating and moving past migration's duality.[22]

Serial migration is not an outsourcing of the self with the aim of developing a less costly or more refined product through the shifting of an object to a location where certain operations and techniques have been perfected or can be had at a lower rate of investment.[23] The decision to change homelands may arise as a strategy for accumulating new outlooks or resources, whether economic or linguistic or social. But making a life of several homelands leads to complex problems that cannot be reduced to an accounting of capital or accumulated experiences. One must progressively engage the various selves that one is, has been, or might yet become. Even under restrictive economic or political conditions, moments of experimentation characterize this process.

In the fourth chapter, I examine how, in a world in which economic logics are often seen as providing global continuity, the serial migrant inscribes her story in political terms. Far from seeking significance in the free flow of media or objects, the migrant bears the border within herself; she is made of the "old maps" that liberal circulation and free exchange would do without. While history marches forward, the migrant might return to where she lived previously, allowing a measure of suppleness in a single life. But this flexibility comes at a price. One's life history may appear disconnected from the chronicle of any public world. Tying together a life across successive homes might seem an interesting exercise, but its full significance might be obscured even to the serial migrant because it seems so idiosyncratic.

Serial migrants rarely voice concerns about how settling in a new homeland might require them to choose to assimilate, integrate, or otherwise set aside their inherited dispositions. Instead, they speak of being haunted by the absence of the measures that have made them in the minds of those among whom they live at present. Anyone might feel nostalgic for the past, regret earlier decisions, or think with longing (or the opposite) of times when alternative measures of worth prevailed, but these feelings take on special salience for those of us who weave our lives of several homelands because the distinct systems of value that lead to such questions have not been foisted upon us by history but rather have come to us, at least to some extent, through our own actions. In the fifth chapter I note how this sense of absence relates to issues of misrecognition. The experience of repeated migration leads the subject to seek continuity both by coming to terms with changes and by willfully challenging herself to take them on. Skills learned and professions practiced are often shed when one shifts from one set of institutional or cultural guidelines to another.

Serial migrants engage some of the most persistent myths of the modern world by using borders to make themselves and to tell the story of their lives. They "redirect" these in tropes that may have tragic as often as ironic implications.[24] But while they insist on the importance of the lines between states to their self-making, and employ essentialized notions of culture as a means of self-clarification, patterns of social interaction that cross borders enable serial migrants to find some comfort not only in particular kinds of "hangouts" but among what one interviewee called "like-minded people." Although they highlight systematic differences in their homelands, they also speak about how certain kinds of places everywhere make them feel immediately at home. In chapter five, I draw on my own previous research to argue that this sense of ease arises because of regularities of social interaction that traverse borders.

The way that shared languages and cultural references enable communication and a sense of familiarity, fostering networks or the development of transnational social formations, is easy to observe. In trying to account for "global" culture it is reasonable to seek out similarly tangible indications of the worldwide adoption or adaption of habits of consumption or tastes: the spread of Starbucks, for instance, or the way a global style is interpreted by local fashion houses. The homogenization of culture, and the arrangements, appropriations, and frictions between the global and the local, have been the focus of research on this subject. My study of beauty salons in Casablanca, Paris, and Cairo departed from these models because it focused on the salon as a site of socialization. I identified three types of salon, each with a distinct pattern of social interaction that fostered specific ways of evaluating fashion, other people, and one's own actions. In the salon one learned how to be with others at the same time one learned to reflect on oneself and the world. But even in a single city, depending on which salon one enters, one learns to be oneself and see the world differently. To enter a proximate, fast, or celebrity salon is to learn to be a part of an entire world. Since these types of salons (and schoolrooms, cafés, offices, and the like) co-exist in a single city and in different measures across countries, serial migrants who do not speak the language of a new country might easily find a home in such social settings; their familiarity with these transnational modes of interaction make it easy to fit in. They might select a place of residence because one of these "worlds" is dominant in the new place, indicating a conception of society or politics that is incipient in ideological debates. In chapter five, I use this "three-world" model to examine continuities in the social life of serial migrants.

Far from turning serial migrants into the disloyal drifters some might imagine inveterate travelers to be, a lifetime of moving on often leads to the formation of especially strong attachments to particular things and other people. In the final chapter I turn Bachelard away from his solitary fixation on walls and drawers and shells toward a poetics of attachment. I decipher words of love and friendship in life stories. I disentangle family ties among those with whom I have worked for many years to notice how serial migration leads to new ways of knotting those ties together. I examine how places and life stages are sewn together and how families and groups of friends who become like kin make collaborative decisions about points of settlement.

I listen to serial migrants not because they are statistically significant or because they represent the wave of the future (although I would wager that their numbers are increasing); rather, I follow them—or us—at first simply to point out that we exist, and subsequently because I believe that our lives, fashioned of some of the basic materials with which the world shapes the big picture of itself, provide a special slant on certain political conundrums.[25] By using bordered territories to set out the evolving backgrounds of lives, serial migrants do more than remind us that, like all images, our maps of the world are made of motion.[26] Their efforts to develop evolving life locations illuminate the fact that although states are increasingly detached from the idea that their sphere of operation is limited to a bounded territory, their sovereignty over certain lands remains vital to their survival. Increasingly, they conceive of their territories both as places of permanent settlement by nationals and as spaces that can be used to carry out projects involving the temporary importation of industries and people for precise intervals.

In focusing on a particular form of settlement punctuated by borders, I hope this book will contribute in some small way to a better understanding of this evolving dance of social life. Anthropologists are perhaps uniquely poised to explore this unfolding politics because to pursue such trails of investigation requires patience of the kind that ethnography encourages. Nonetheless, in the coming pages the reader will find little of the "thick description" that has become the trademark of ethnographic writing; in this exploration of an evolving location I myself inhabit, biographical revelation is conspicuously absent. This "try" at delineating a trail for which there is no map, no sign, no frame, this account of a way of life with no content except the form, may seem to have little to do with the task of disentangling the webs of cultures we might appreciate as outsiders. It dwells instead on how a shared experience might result from using a common compass rather than inhabiting a common space or speaking a shared language. Neither the naked eye nor the geneticist will come up with traits these people have in common. I might myself feel nostalgic for that delicate attention to the intricacies of symbolic exchange that leads the participant observer to notice each slight variation in a tone of voice, turn each ritual gesture into a sign, make each aside in a conversation a reminder of the deep significance of a shared belief or a subtle indication of divergent opinion. Yet in this work about lives so full of significant details that one might easily be overwhelmed, a paucity of illustration is consonant with the subject matter. This "path-ology" requires an emphasis on form at the expense of content.

CHAPTER I

COSMOPOLITAN CONTENT

Efforts to define the cosmopolitan have been at the center of recent debates about world politics, new forms of culture, and human rights. Is he a product of the global market or a reflection of the growth of transnational political connections? Is she a member of an emerging elite or a product of a new world culture? An ever-growing literature seeks to define this elusive figure. But whether we picture the cosmopolitan as a concerned world citizen in a Greenpeace T-shirt asking for donations or a businessman in an Armani suit engaged in a conference call in an airport lounge, whether we seek to include the exile or the world-music performer in this global portrait gallery, all we can know for sure about the cosmopolitan is that disengagement is her defining feature.[1]

The cosmopolitan moves from settled ideas or societies or cultures toward a freedom born of a widening of political perspectives and cultural imaginations. Her gravity-defying performance might be understood as a critique of prevalent assumptions about our being the product of the social worlds we are born into. Through him we seek to recognize that societies have grown beyond the nation, to form outlooks that are not mired in received opinion, to account for global connections made possible by the intensification of exchange and travel associated with globalization. The movement toward a cosmopolitan consciousness leads to a distanced way of looking at what holds people together at their most universal. A movement toward anywhere creates the cosmopolitan's allure.[2]

Cosmopolitans are defined by a mental disposition, bringing to mind Georg Simmel's account of "individualistic persons" who

> with their qualitative determinacy and the unmistakability of their life contents, therefore resist incorporation into an order that is valid for everyone, in which they would have a calculable position according to a consistent principle. Conversely, where the organization of the whole regulates the achievement of the individual according to an end not located within him or herself, then their position must be fixed according to an external system. It is not an inner or ideal norm but rather the relationship to the totality that secures this position, which is therefore most suitably determined by a numerical arrangement.[3]

If cosmopolitanism can be understood as a movement to reassess the "inner and ideal norms" that organize the world system and inform an inchoate global culture, we might follow this figure in his many forms to conceive a politics of the future.[4] But by what means of transportation might we embark on this journey? The relationship of physical displacement to the cosmopolitan's critical disengagement is a point of contention. Many assume that some experience of international travel is what makes the cosmopolitan worldly. But others claim that being swept up in flows of images and information about distant lands suffices to lift someone out of a context she has inherited, setting her on the road to the disengaged appreciation and deliberation typical of the cosmopolitan individual.[5] In either case, we should be suspicious of the very idea that one might leap in a single bound from what is given to everyone, to what we should hope for. What place does the cosmopolitan move away from? What generates the momentum of her motion? A flight toward the cosmos is taken to signal the individual's freedom from the gravity of tradition and to step beyond the narrow confines of nationalism. But how might the cosmopolitan know when he has reached a resting point from which to observe his own progress? At which moment might he decide to ponder his position? Some suggest that "cosmopolitan virtue" involves a distancing related to modes of Socratic irony. But are there not various kinds of distance and manners of achieving it?[6]

The cosmopolitan's remoteness from the grounds of social experience has led to accusations that those who seek the politics of the future in the development of the cosmopolitan subject have imagined her as a reflection of their own intellectualism. Vernacular, ordinary, not to mention "abject" cosmopolitans have been devised or recognized in response to these criticisms; these qualifications seem to render the link between forms of life and forms of consciousness more precise.[7] Yet hyphenation simply underscores the value attributed to the term of reference. While recognizing the good intentions of those who seek to expand the cosmopolitan to those whose image rarely comes to mind when we conjure up this worldly figure, we must consider the fundamental deference that amending the cosmopolitan implies. The cosmopolitan's conceit is born less of ethnocentrism or class position than a failure to see that his claim to novelty is a rendition on a well-known song, an old standard composed during the Enlightenment. A two-step contrast of settlement to airy flight sets the tempo for the distinctive melodies of modern nations and societies. It is in contrast to the unmoving grounds of unconscious, bodily practices associated with the past, the countryside, tradition, and exotic peoples that it develops its progressions.[8] To recognize the continuing power of its cadence is essential, but to understand how it persists in drawing the entire world into its compositional logic might require paying attention to the way its instruments are made and its orchestras assembled.

The cosmopolitan takes the nations of the modern age as her point of departure for taking wing toward a politics of the cosmos. She does not depart from any place, but from a space made of earlier flights. She follows previous generations who have progressively left behind some ground of warm social bonds and inherited culture to join a more abstract, individualized modern society. She mimes the moves of the peasant to the city, the sense of belonging as it moves from the village to the nation, now taking those as her starting point. Following the compelling direction of this displacement from an image of the social world as warm, all embracing, perhaps maternal, she moves yet again, this time distancing herself from the national imaginations that are already the sign of an earlier upheaval. She pulls away from habit to seek some ethereal space from which one might gain a perspective on the world at large.[9] But how does she find the content of her character in this way of moving away from the ground toward the cosmos? Does her face lose its color in the course of this skyward motion? Or, as some writers theorize, does she have the opportunity to collect colors from the world at large to paint her face in hybrid forms of consciously remixed and reassembled patterns? In either case, one must wonder what distinguishes her from those other late-modern subjects that sociologists tell us are increasingly self-reflexive and ecumenical in composing the self, taking a mix-and-match approach, finding meaning in celebrations of personal *bricolage*.[10] How does she select the colors that give her face expression, how does she collect the contents from which she might form her character? What motivates her to select one shade or opinion rather than another?

Nadia Tazi points out that cosmopolitans "permit themselves a certain distance that includes a vanity or perhaps a naiveté, a belief that they are able to understand both sides." Because cosmopolitanism is conceived as a critical distance, "cosmopolitans will naturally feel a great repugnance for Manichaeisms, or the brutal choices imposed by crises. When they feel themselves in a double bind, they either go elsewhere, hopping from a dyschronic point to a consonant one, from a disparity to a comparity, or they must find their balance and mobility through an emotional and intellectual detachment that cuts them apart."[11] The cosmopolitan is aloof: she inhabits a place from which she can contemplate alternatives. But admission to this lofty space seems to require a disconnection not only from the ground but from one's own emotions and the impulses that lead to relationships with actual others.[12] What's more, the lack of definition of what makes up a cosmopolitan condemns him to phrase his critiques in the very cultural and political languages from which the cosmopolitan gaze promises distance.

To conceive figures in motion in opposition to some "absolute ground" encourages us to see those who move as exceptions. It leads us to ignore how states and regions and ideas about the world at large take form and gain in forcefulness because of *how* they construe the ground, not because they are stuck in place. To explore how choreographies of power are related to the backgrounds against which individual faces, bodies, and lives might be projected does not mean discarding paradigms of settling. Rather, it involves moving away from an emphasis on oppositions of territory to mobility and instead concentrating on how and when and why certain backgrounds come to the fore and attending to how ways of moving accompany manners of settling down and making oneself at home. Those who repeat the migration journey observe that family trees can have roots in many places and that states often wage war to consolidate their territory; the image of a nation or the regularities of culture require effort to maintain. They often tell their stories against the background of territorial disputes, lands where the forces of state and settled society are difficult to discern, and places where tongues intermingle.

In a world in motion, it is a sign of privilege to live where the social and political abstractions that guide the way the world at large is imagined seem natural, where place and polity and culture appear seamlessly bound together. This is one of the things that make the idea of a cosmopolitan perspective achieved by distancing oneself from the grounds of social life to appear so narrow-minded and elitist. While many serial migrants seemed to effortlessly embody prevalent images of the sophisticated, tolerant, educated, politically perspicacious cosmopolitan, their stories led me to take note of how the cosmopolitan's pretension is not essentially one of economic or social position or style. It is the cosmopolitan's claim of flying away from what others live through that leads serial migrants to overwhelmingly refuse any association with a figure they tend to perceive as a modern-day Icarus.[13] Those who make their lives across borders find little appeal in a flight to nowhere in particular and see cosmopolitanism as an indication of hubris.

ORIGINAL DISTANCE

When I asked Hélène if she considered herself a cosmopolitan, she laughed and said that she is merely a "Terrian"—a person of the Earth, unable to view it from afar or to escape the forces of gravity. We met in Manama, where she was working as a manager for a software company. She left her native France many years ago to live in Belgium, Senegal, San Francisco. Still, she explained that she hangs on to her origins, weaving her boundary-crossing life from the threads of Paris:

> We [serial migrants] build our own idea of our background. For example, I carry with me this notion that I am Parisian, which has become a sort of cultural idealistic label. It is actually very remote from being a Parisian in Paris. In fact, I cannot relate to what Parisians are today. I could no longer live like they live. The word "Parisian" has different meanings for them and for me.

If truth emerges from statistics gathered at a given place and time, then the way that Hélène uses Paris as a source of continuity for her life story might be seen as involving a good measure of illusion or self-deception. She is the first to explain that her enactment of the Parisian throughout her moves across the world has more to do with her own past than with "how people live in Paris now." She recognizes that those who live today in France's capital are shaping the city in ways that she ignores. She calls her use of Paris as a background to figure herself "culturally idealistic" and thus separates it out from the city as a territory populated by its current inhabitants. When she considers herself a Parisian, she does not move away from a settled place but instead contrasts the idea of the "really lived" to an "ideal" form of figuration, invoking a manner of taking one's distance from the street, the nation, and one's own natural body that is integral to the figure of the *Parisienne*, a highly gendered figure of a type of woman who has learned to take a certain distance from the idea that a person is simply a product of a natural or social milieu.

Over a century ago Louis Octave Uzanne wrote that "a woman may be *Parisienne* by taste and instinct . . . in any town or country in the world," yet "fully five sixths of the women in Paris" were "provincial in spirit and manners."[14] A distance from the idea of the natural body marks modern beauties around the world; a step away from the land and one's birth culture sets the steps of the modern dance that the cosmopolitan takes to a new level of perfection. A "Parisienne" evolves with reference to a specific city that is varied and changing, an image as much as an environment. She incorporates a distinctive distance from the populace and the street, which themselves are defined in contrast to the "natural" body of the peasant, the savage, or the immigrant who has come to the city from some far-off native place, and her own unfashioned corporality.

Anyone from anywhere might become Parisian, but for a woman to show herself to be a Parisienne she must be willing to work with a particular understanding of the city, of culture, and self-cultivation. To take on this identity involves following a consistent principle.

This principle is not independent of the content of the place, but the content is not grounded in some fundamental way; rather, it is tethered to a specific ground through multiple mediations. Indeed, the Parisienne could be considered a critical demonstration of the determination to break with the idea that a person is simply a product of an unconsciously transmitted *habitus*, a singular emanation of some natural cultural context. This "idealized cultural label" is defined and limited by reference to a particular ideal of the city and to a specific metropolis. It is a reminder of the importance of place but also of the fact that places, like images, are made of movement as much as some grounded physical and cultural substance. The Parisienne reverses the idea of the universal as expressed in a movement between a singular place or way of life and a set of global possibilities.

Hélène walks with reference to the capital of France even while she roams the world. She has lived in Brussels, San Francisco, Dakar, and Manama. She explains that drawing herself with the pencil of Paris offers protection from the danger of "getting too involved." The Parisienne's "detachment" from the natural social body means that she, like Hélène, is able to "avoid becoming too caught up in political or social causes in any single place." This clinging to Paris might be interpreted as a symptom of a lack of cosmopolitanism, the Parisian herself a failed effort to see the world from a wider perspective, an attachment to a certain cultural ideology, economic and social status, or political order.

Wherever Hélène has lived, she has been troubled by the inequalities and injustices she observes: poverty in Dakar, racism in the United States, and the "caste system" that reigns in the Gulf countries profoundly disturb her. By tying her life together with the threads of Paris, she says that she can "maintain a certain distance" from those who suffer. The distance from her own "nature" and emotions that she learned by becoming a Parisienne makes tolerable her inability to fight the injustices she observes in each of her homelands. Hélène's pain does not arise from being torn between points of view or ideologies; Hélène is not sure, but thinks that her depth of feeling might arise from her "left-leaning" politics, the persistence of ideals set while she was growing up in a country where calls for *liberté*, *egalité*, and *fraternité* are ever present. Although she insists that hanging on to herself as a Parisienne helps her to "avoid involvement," a distance may be necessary precisely because she assumes a certain understanding of equality, a certain universal set of principles about justice. Not only might this indicate that she is especially aware of inequality as expressed in position or status, or that she is conscious of her own good luck at being born into the French middle class, but it might also lead one to imagine that as an individual someone should ideally be able to take action anywhere. Yet how is this possible? It is difficult even to imagine a form of charity or political action that can cross several borders and remain effective, and nearly impossible to develop a political conversation in several languages according to such a cosmopolitan ideal.[15] Helen's conundrum points to the real challenges of developing a cosmopolitics and the limits of imagining solutions in terms of a cosmopolitan subject. In this sense, the elitism or ordinariness of the cosmopolitan subject is irrelevant.

Hélène's city of origin is more than a point of reference: it is a way to protect herself from dwelling on actions she has not taken. She says that her "distance of origin" helps her cope with what she is unable to change—for example, diverse systems' ways of discriminating against different types of people. In San Francisco she saw racism; in Senegal, poverty. In Bahrain she has had to live with the way in which national identities dictate people's economic function, mobility and social life. She herself is reduced to being a European or a manager, separating her inexorably from the Indian shopkeeper or Filipino maid. She also notes that political power is held by a minority, even among those of the population who are citizens. The majority of the population are Shia but a Sunni dynasty rules the country. Being Parisienne enables her to move following a consistent set of principles even as she participates in different systems.

Hélène's attachment to her origins enables her to move forward. Paris guides her steps even as the particular forms of distance it has taught her cause her to renounce the idea that she might act to make a difference in the places she inhabits. Her example suggests to us that settling in one country instead of another might encourage an awareness of the lack of power of the individual who rises above the usual grounds of social intercourse. Her difficulties arise not from critical distance and the difficulty of choosing a position but rather because she recognizes how maintaining subjective continuity across very different environments might require one to learn to instinctively take a step back not from a "context" but from one's own initial emotional response to it. This habit of taking a distance from one's own potential for empathy and action might be a condition for maintaining the "left-leaning ideals" that Hélène says make her uneasy about her inability to act against the injustices she observes or experiences.

IMPOSSIBLE FLIGHTS

Since Hélène's attachment to Paris smoothes her pathway around the world without causing her to question the "inner and ideal norms" of her place of origin, we might think that issues of cosmopolitanism are beside the point in addressing her situation. But what of people whose stories show that shrugging off the bounds of national origin was fundamental to their desire to migrate? And what of those who explain that their motivation for gaining perspective on the world are expressly tied to political ideals that are different from the ideals they were exposed to as children?

Laurence, another serial migrant from a middle-class family, explained that his motivations for leaving the UK were explicitly political. He attended a boarding school in Cornwall; when he ventured into the village pub, working-class boys saw him as an easy target. From these regular beatings he realized the importance of class distinctions to British society and he developed, as he put it, "a virulent hatred of the British class system." As soon as he turned eighteen he left the UK to settle in Calgary, and he became a Canadian citizen. But a few years later he decided to rethink his ties to England and to "test" life there as an adult. He moved to London to study printmaking and obtain a teaching degree. But that was in the 1980s; Margaret Thatcher was at the height of her reign. He found living in a country ruled according to her conservative, free-trade ideology intolerable and decided to leave again, heading this time for Japan.[16] He lived there for nearly a decade, first in Tokyo and then in the countryside near Nagasaki, where he met the woman who would become his wife. Together they decided to try living in Germany, but his wife thought it was too cold and gray and found the people inhospitable. When he was offered a teaching job in sunny Bahrain, they were both happy to move again.

He told me that over the years he has come to consider the ability to change countries and jobs at will as a necessary freedom. He noted that he has had the privilege of moving with relative ease, and that many people don't. But then he cautioned me that although he has strong opinions about politics, I should not assume he has any pretensions of "doing good" in the world; he does not. Detachment from the UK is indeed a result of his political convictions, but his life of "floating" from place to place has not put him in a position to act on them. He is able to move so freely because his path is paved by the language of colonial and capitalist expansion. It troubles him that as a teacher in English-language schools he "indoctrinates" others into a language and a way of thinking that he himself fled, yet he has made few efforts to learn other languages. Even though he lived in Japan for many years, he still speaks only enough Japanese to "get by." In the Gulf countries, English is the lingua franca. In his monolingual world he can have the kinds of in-depth conversations that take most people years to approximate in a language learned as an adult. He has the option of being a considerate listener and teacher to non-native speakers while drawing spontaneously on his mastery of the tongue to settle a contract or win an argument. He recognizes the potential for condescension in such relationships, a shadowy reflection of what might be taken to be a cosmopolitan concern for others.

Laurence is a photographer. Indeed, he says he prefers to encounter people through the frame of his lens. His camera helps him to avoid "engaging people at all levels."[17] He likes to observe others and capture their gestures without having to talk to them. He sees his refusal to imagine himself "absorbed" in the "local culture" as both realistic and principled. Ultimately he wants to move away from people altogether, to return to Canada and retire to the far North, where interactions with others would be limited. But for now he is thinking about moving to Paris, of all places! I ask Laurence about his desire to move to a crowded urban center where it is notoriously difficult to get by without speaking the language. Are his motivations financial? "It's not about money," he tells me. "It is too simple to assume that people move for money." In fact, at his current job his salary is lower than it was in Germany. Then what could possibly motivate him to move to Paris? "It is because of my daughter," he explains.

Laurence proudly tells me that his three-year-old girl speaks flawless Japanese and perfect English. Now, he wants her to learn French. As he speaks of the advantages of early language acquisition, the icy, ironic edge of his voice melts. He is not sure whether staying put or moving around is best for his child, but he is convinced that he must contemplate limiting his freedom of motion if it is best for her future. As I listen, I begin to understand his efforts to detach himself from the politics of class by leaving England as a movement that cannot be understood in terms of an individual action. His flight, the distance he seeks through the lens of his camera, the alienated, misanthropic persona he presents, all take on new meaning once he speaks about his hopes for educating his daughter. While he lives in a world limited to English in spite of his travels, he seeks to set her free of the prison house of language. Through her he acts to counter the pretension of those who would heal the world's problems by assimilating everyone to some universal standard, a leveling that requires people to submit to a common economic system and a politics dominated by the ideas that led him to abandon England, only to find the system he detests prevailing everywhere, and to find himself part of the effort to promote the dissemination of its instrument, his mother tongue.[18]

Imagining his child's future provides Laurence's life a new horizon. Through her, he might see his own movements take form and make sense. Unlike her father, she may not take up a camera to get a perspective on different ways of life from a distance. She might not come to know isolation as the price of freedom of movement because she will be able to engage with people in their own idiom. Laurence's concern for where he should settle his child might seem to flow into clichés about immigrants who leave their homelands and sacrifice themselves for the next generation. Yet he does not point his daughter in the direction of some wealthier nation, somewhere where she might "get ahead" in a globally conceived hierarchy of wealth and status. Instead, he conceives of her having conversations in formerly influential languages that have lost their regional or international role to English. Of course, he must teach her English if he hopes to speak with her, but might it not be more forward-thinking to do as some upper-class parents in North America do and have her study Chinese? The path he opens to her extends his own dream of leaving behind class divisions and the status of a powerful language and educational system toward an appreciation of other ways of life, manners of living he can only appreciate from afar.[19]

Laurence's serial migrations might be construed as an effort to achieve the critical distance typical of a cosmopolitan subject, but he shows that the freedom to go anywhere can make moving from one place to another problematic.[20] He draws an ironic portrait of himself as a person who is "concerned" about culture, yet he observes others through the lens of his camera. They are pure visions and he can consider them from varied perspectives, but like the indecisive cosmopolitan of Tazi's depiction, he must always have trouble deciding which point of view to adopt as his own. It is only as a father that he begins to get a sense of how certain values or hopes might lead him to choose a direction, and even then he explains that this decision causes him a certain ambivalence, because for all of his dedication to his child, to move or stay for her involves a "loss of freedom." Still, noticing how his voice deepens as he imagines his daughter's future, I reflect on the fact that while cosmopolitical debates imply the importance of saving the world for "future generations," stories of "becoming cosmopolitan" often involve long dissertations on one's parents. They seldom mention how our own moves are often determined by the concrete worlds we hope to create for our children.[21]

ORIGINS DISPLACED

As I enter the Ouadahi home in Laval, I am greeted by multilingual chatter:

> Jamal! Finek? Aji Salim, let me tie your shoes, as tu terminé tes devoirs? ¿Dónde está tu hermana? Elle parle au téléphone. Maman je suis là! smati weldi, khass nemshiou daba, Maman attends-moi! Jamal, est-qu'il reste assez d'œufs? What about al hlib? Anyway, on y va y'alla, bye bye!

Family members contributed differently to the warp and woof of this sound material made up of Moroccan Arabic, French, English, and Spanish. I notice that Leila often speaks Moroccan Arabic (*derija*) to her son and English with her daughter. She explains that her intention is not some random "incorporation" of languages as a reproduction of some "native" soundscape, but because each of her children "needs practice" in a different tongue. Selim, who was born in Quebec, "*should learn*" Arabic to talk to the family. Yasmine's English is good, but why not get a little more practice? She may decide to move to Ontario or Vancouver or New York one day. To some extent, the texture of talk is a reminder of how people speak in Morocco. But the sounds that fill the house are also the result of decisions about how language can be a strategic tool shaping the children's future. The particular mix of tongues creates a space of intimacy: it is a way of including each individual in the ongoing family story. For Leila to speak English is to recall the years she spent in England in her twenties. Talking with Yasmine in Spanish, she mimics her own parents' practice, using the distinctive syncopation of the Moroccan dialect laced with Spanish to reanimate cherished memories of taking the boat between Morocco and Spain with her father.

Leila was born in 1960 into a modest family in Tangiers. Her father was a city policeman; her mother is illiterate but speaks several languages. Leila attended French schools almost by chance and then attended university in Toulouse. There, she studied languages, earning a master's degree in translation; she also met and married Jamal and gave birth to her daughter, Yasmine. Leila and Jamal established themselves in France as permanent immigrants at about the same time that a visa came into effect for Moroccans wishing to travel to Europe. Not coincidentally, the late 1980s marked the rise of the National Front Party and the development of immigration as a major theme of political debate and social tension throughout Europe.[22] Jamal, who is from Fez, felt especially vulnerable as an "Arab" in France. By 1990, when I met them, they had relocated to Rabat. But once there, they did not feel settled. Leila reflected on this in a text she wrote for the Georgetown seminar:

> I always thought being born in Tangiers was a great privilege. But one day, everything changed. I realized that what has always been seen as an international city had suddenly been remapped to become a city of the Arab world. Tangiers where we spoke so many languages, where no

borders made any difference, the city to which people came from the Rif mountains and from what is called the "interior" of Morocco as well as from all of the ports of the Mediterranean, my dear Tangiers was being abruptly closed, cordoned off from its natural setting. From Tangiers you cannot see Cairo or Jeddah, but Algeciras is clearly visible on the horizon. It is this geography of a Tangiers linked to these places that is natural to me. But Europe decided that the natural geography I grew up with simply wasn't right. In the 1980s visas were imposed for those who wanted to cross the straits of Gibraltar from the south. The mapmakers, border guards and consulate administrators reconceived Tangiers as a kind of Western outpost of the Arab world. This set me on a path of serial migration. It led me to develop a kind of errant nostalgia for my city that has sent me out to search for a space resembling the one in which I was raised.[23]

While some serial migrants use their birthplace as a ribbon to tie their lives together, others have seen history erase their birthplace from the map. States disappear. Borders shift. Hometowns are joined to new countries. Leila writes that the Tangiers where she grew up "no longer exists" because of a changing importance of regional frontiers. This is what led her to decide to leave Morocco with her family a second time and settle in Quebec.

Leila conceives of Tangiers as tied to a region that unfolds as one looks out across the water toward Spain and beyond. The Mediterranean is a sea but also a region and an ideal whose name intimates continuities of cultural practice across religious, linguistic, and political divides.[24] The sea is invoked by southern European leaders when they seek to maintain political influence in North Africa and the Levant. But it also serves as a reference point for those on its southern shore who seek to emphasize their ties to the secular and democratic states on the other side. This is a region not of particular languages but of a culture that follows the contours of the land. To mention the Mediterranean is to connote an ecumenism in opposition to fundamentalism's claim to exclusive interpretations of singular texts and a single sacred tongue.

Leila's choice of Tangiers as the background that animates both her movements and modes of dwelling is strategic. Her manner of animating "her" Tangiers in everyday interactions is a comment on an evolving situation in the present. Memories are brought to mind by ongoing struggles to locate Tangiers, Morocco, and Leila herself. The texture of sound in the Ouadahi household is not a vestige or a souvenir. It is a part of an effort to promote a set of political choices. She militates against the claims of a linguistically defined "Arab world," offering up the sounds of her home not as some random collection or an ill-defined hybrid, but as a deliberate composition. If one listens carefully, it becomes apparent that while Quebecois words are expressed in the accents of France, and languages mingle, the Arabic is strictly colloquial; even if it includes—thanks to Jamal—a spattering of Fassi inflections and terms, there is no hint of the classical language that joins the Arab world, no echo of the words that have been introduced to everyday Moroccan talk by Egyptian film and song or pan-Arab television. Leila's recipe for talk is at once a recollection of the sounds of her childhood and a political program that does not admit just any kind of mixture. Her conversations with her spouse and children (and with me when I am visiting) are an appeal to a certain social reality. In their daily reenactment they propose a theory of culture and an understanding of history that takes unconscious dispositions and practices as its grounding.[25] Against the claims of an Arab world with formal grammar, in contrast to the association of a nation with a single tongue, she directs the patter of syllables to evoke the continuity of a landscape that extends to her living room in Laval. Her image of Tangiers without borders is suggestive of the nomad who moves in tune with the land, finding himself at home wherever he goes because he makes a region of his travels, a milieu of his roving body.

CHAPTER 2

NOMADIC ACTION

W HILE THE COSMOPOLITAN achieves definition by taking a critical distance from what
others take for granted, the nomad's difference arises from a moving
harmony of land and body. Gilles Deleuze and Felix Guattari con-
figure this peripatetic figure as a performer of an effortless dance that
transforms the abstraction and divisions of the modern world into a
smooth continuum. Whether portrayed as a member of a marauding
band or as a roving king of a premodern realm, this nomad presses
ever onward; a potentially destructive force with an unlimited appetite, he recognizes no borders; he is a concept, a mirage, a mode of
operation. He is a self-enclosed war machine that follows the land's
contours to turn the state's energies against itself; he is a permanent
threat to the state's efforts to maintain itself through strategies of
containment, its struggle to maintain a fixed order within set boundaries. The nomad does not explain the transformations he effects: indeed, he is bereft of any communicative code.[1] He might thus seem a
mysteriously attractive alternative to the talkative cosmopolitan, his
silent progress an antidote to her never-ending talk about the bor-

derless worlds of tomorrow, his every gesture a silent summons to a politics of direct action.[2]

The nomad's refusal to negotiate with settled orders has intrigued writers and philosophers who see in him more than a representative of a current of thought or an ideology. The nomad is a moving process, a mode of operation enmeshed in the movement of the body.[3] Those entranced by this concept variously imagine that it might enable a more dynamic comprehension of the movement of history or people; one might come to recognize a wider range of ways of inhabiting the Earth and how moving subjects challenge static social orders and settled ways of thought. The nomad takes shape in opposition to the way that the state seeks to settle the migrant, establish hierarchical societies, and direct the flows of goods or information. Deleuze and Guattari call this "striation."[4] In seeking to stake out the claims of mobile forms of life in opposition to settled conceptions of dwelling promoted by the state's striating agenda, Edward S. Casey sees in the nomad's "local integration" a paradigmatic shift that is "effected by the moving body, which is the bearer of an unhoused inhabitation, the very vehicle of space without conduits or settled sites." Casey continues:

> The result is a peculiar but important form of dwelling that breaks
> with the paradigm of the settled, to which Heidegger and Bachelard
> still cling. Nor is it a matter of the unhomely, the literally *unheimlich*,
> within the home; the nomad is perfectly at home on the desert or the
> steppe; nothing is uncanny there. Instead, it is a matter of continual
> deterritorialization of the land, converting it into the absolute ground of
> an ongoing journey.[5]

To depict the nomad as a revolt against settlement is to adopt the same opposition of stasis to mobility as those individuals whose idea of beauty is a still life composed of fruit that never withers and those institutions that conceive of peace as a state where everything has a place and every person a clear position. The nomad might appear a sensual alternative to cosmopolitan abstraction, tolerance, and civility.

However, this specter of capitalism's dialectic, this apparent source of transformation, evolves according to set oppositions of territory to landscape, culture to nature, and mobility to stasis that his chatty double, the cosmopolitan, is at least willing to negotiate, blur, or relativize. Perhaps the nomad's progress is alluring to some thinkers precisely because it obscures how nomadic peoples engage the state by avoiding borders and how states get themselves entangled in the striating processes of other states, international agencies, or powerful corporations.[6]

Obtuse nomads, like savvy cosmopolitans, claim to challenge settled political and social orders: one through distanced contemplation and polite conversations aimed at civic action, the other through embodied action. Their politics diverge, yet they share a similar understanding of the background against which their ideas and their actions might be projected. The notion that the Earth can be smoothly converted into an absolute ground is appealing for those who insist on the erosion of state power in an era of global flows. It is equally attractive to some who envision meetings with others as a creative alternative to the constraints of closed cultures. Deleuze and Guattari explain:

> One of the fundamental tasks of the State is to striate the space over
> which it reigns, or to utilise smooth spaces as a means of communication
> in the service of striated spaces. It is a vital concern of every State
> not only to vanquish nomadism but to control migrations and, more
> generally, to establish a zone of rights over an entire "exterior," over all of
> the flows of the ecumenon. If it can help it the State does not dissociate
> itself from a process of capture of flows of all kinds, populations,
> commodities or commerce, money or capital, etc.[7]

But might this concept be best able to illuminate the intricacies of state action if it is set free from a singular opposition of striation to nomadic flow and the intimate connection they imagine between the state and its territory? Might their conception of the state itself be too fixed to take into account the location and modes of operation of both states and individual wanderers and the variety of paths that make each of these a generalization about various distinct types of subjects?

States, like nomads, are made in motion. Their wealth depends on shifting investments in fluid markets. They plunge in the currents of global communication to produce their image.[8] They do not act alone to direct the flows of migration or trade, but in concert with commercial enterprises, other states, and international agencies that aid or hinder their efforts to draw up and secure their borders. Like individuals, states may share systems of belief or language with one another. They may have family connections, or common military and economic interests. They get entangled with other states' efforts at striation and transform these other states' actions in ways that can be called nomadic. Is not the state always on an "ongoing journey," a subject that sometimes struggles to maintain itself? States have diverse relationships to their territories. They can conceive them as terrains of permanent settlement, as work houses or passageways. They sometimes use their power to create nomads. Their inability to striate their lands or their lack of negotiation with other states unsettles millions of people.

People departing from their places of origin may traverse forbidding deserts and navigate treacherous seas, landscapes where borders are unmarked. But they cannot ignore the state even as they elude its grasp; their wanderlust does not protect them from the extortions of *passeurs* or the requirement that they offer *baksheesh* to the hungry police that feed off borders. In the world of today, what could be worse than being stateless? Even those whose passports enable them to pass checkpoints with confidence suffer the questions of border guards and endure background checks; their fingerprints or iris patterns are recorded, their credit-card purchases followed to chart the direction of their peregrinations. Travelers may evade the settling action of a state, but for all of their desire and hunger and their ceaseless displacements, they do not transform anything, least of all themselves.

The young men from Albania and North Africa who have been followed by Nick Mai as they traveled across the newly open spaces of the European Union might seem to be caught up in a nomadic mimesis.[9] Like Mai himself, who left his small Italian town for London, they found inspiration for their migrations in the beautiful images of elsewhere they encountered in movies or television series. Listening to music from far-off lands, they imagined themselves as pop stars or superheroes; listening to their elders, they learned that migration is a story of going to a land of big bucks, big cars, and blond wives. What's more, big European cities appeared as a space of personal liberation from the strict expectations of what life should be like for a young man in a small town, in a patriarchal society, in a poor country. And so they depart. They wander the borderless space set out by the Schengen Convention. They do not stop because they never seem to arrive at their destination, that El Dorado of the electronic imagination. Their aversion to remaining in places that do not offer the riches they expect in return for their migratory investment leaves them literally unable to settle.

Fleeing the state's police officers and social workers, these youths are easy prey for traffickers of all kinds. Their lives become eternal one-night stands because they remain attached to conceptions of migratory success that are current in the homelands they flee. Indeed, their movements seem to tie them ever more tightly to the expectations and ideas of masculinity that they sought to escape through migration. Their refusal to settle leaves them with no alternative; they have no set image of themselves, no alternative way of life to oppose to this original frame of reference, just as they possess no material evidence of the value of their uprooting. Mai interprets this form of life in psychological terms, suggesting that these "errant" young men live suspended in adolescence. If they had settled in, found a job, attended school, they might have developed other notions of the good life or a good man than those they associated with their places of origin. These men who disregard borders and dodge the forces that would settle them are not freed of their birthplaces by their mobility but instead are tethered ever more tightly to their point of departure. They elude the expectations of men current in their place of origin only by evading them.[10] For them, wandering across unmarked landscapes is indeed "revolutionary," a revolving door that returns them to the point of departure.

Other would-be nomads languish in border zones. In 2005, not far from Tangiers, migrants from sub-Saharan Africa and beyond gathered in camps outside the Spanish enclaves of Ceuta and Melilla.[11] These young men do not travel to elude the grasp of the state. On the contrary, they hope to settle in a state more prosperous or more democratic, or simply different from the one they left. These bands of wanderers are not solitary; they often travel in groups to cross the Sahara. They do not move in harmony with landscapes but organize their settlements in the Moroccan forest according to national origin, divvying out tasks to these national ensembles and collaborating to maintain order and hygiene. Selected individuals represent their constituents in the collective deliberations of this sylvan "United Nations."[12] They all share a single goal: to scale the fence and set foot on European soil. Accomplishing the goal involves a sudden change in status: one becomes subject to European laws and gains a hearing that might enable one to become a refugee, an exile, or an immigrant. Despite the different possible endings to their stories, they act in the border zone with a sense of a common cause. Even in the absence of the state, in the shadow of the walls of "fortress Europe," their actions are not simply mimetic with respect to the coordinating, striating effects of the state and the international system of nation-states; they include notions of sacrifice and the common good suggestive of national sentiment.[13] In the way that they collectively storm the fences that mark the border, they demonstrate a sense of selfless action reminiscent of the national feeling that sends young men and women to battle. They advance en masse to create chaos, enabling a few lucky ones to make it to the other side. Each individual knows that his own chances are slim, and many are injured or killed in their efforts.[14] Yet they engage in a collective project, triumphing each time one of them sets foot in Europe.

Wanderers entranced by a mirage of wealth and liberation assure a process of eternal return to their points of origin by eschewing settlement. People stopped in their tracks by borders "striate" the spaces they temporarily inhabit by reference to a politics of the nation-state. When states themselves often act in nomadic fashion, it seems difficult to explain the circulations of people or the movements of the world in terms of a nomad/state dialectic. The nomad amazes us by gliding over the Earth, but the life threads of those who live across borders are snagged by state bureaucracies. The fabric of their lives is woven of the threads of habits that are not just theirs but those of the world at large. If one were to imagine a nomad incarnate, a truly transformative subject, might it be in the form of someone claimed by several states, or none, a being born in some cosmopolitan heaven, unable to experience a longing for the land left behind, a serial migrant by birth and choice?

LANDING PATTERNS

Tameem's mother is from Scotland, his father from Bahrain. Both of his parents were diplomats, and he was brought up in many different countries. As an adult he settled first in New York City and then in Paris, where his French wife still lives with their daughter. By 2004 or 2005 he was working as an architect in Bahrain and investing in real estate, buying land where—as he puts it—he could afford it. Among other places, he owns land in Pennsylvania, Romania, Bahrain, and the California desert. His long-term goal is of course to turn a profit. But what strikes me as especially interesting is the formula he uses to guide his purchases. He finds sitting on a commercial jet very uncomfortable;

a flight of more than six hours is intolerable. So he plots out his domain in such a way that he can find a flight that takes no more than six hours to get him from one of his territories to another. That is his mode of operation.

I try to visualize a map of the world drawn up following his six-hour procedure; I recall hearing news reports about UN votes to establish no-fly zones on the evening news. I plot out US military bases and compare the way that news agencies "cover" the world by making a savvy selection of locations for their bureaus. Tameem's imaginative strategy is set not by evaluating theaters of potential conflict or getting journalists to locations where stories are breaking; rather, it is computed according to a calculus of bodily comfort. His six-hour rule for purchases of land works with the map of the world to envision a particular body (his own) set in motion in an orderly fashion. His fantasy of construing a region in tune with his body clock may bring to mind the nomad's self-enclosed independence, yet the map of this domain is not synchronized with the rhythms of nature. It takes little notice of the lay of the land. Instead, it conceives of space in terms of the times of schedules and flight patterns set up by airline companies, state bureaucracies, and international contracts. He uses airports and freeway systems, airlines and shuttle buses, to formulate a domain calculated in intervals of time set according to a personal measure of corporal tolerance.

Tameem says that his way of setting out the map of the world by measuring its territories as intervals of time in the air must be a way of reacting to a lack of what people call "roots." He cannot feel uprooted, he insists; from which ground would he have been disengaged? Which place or group might claim him? He cautions me not to consider this a "problem." For him it is simply a fact. Almost from birth he found himself wondering where he would move next, seeking direction on maps, moving through countries in succession. As the child of diplomats, each representing a different state, his periodic shifts of habitation took place within a milieu in which people move with their countries and represent them wherever they travel. His family was bifurcated with respect to the national point of reference but unified in its belonging to this diplomatic mode of operation. Yet they remained within a single social medium in spite of displacements, with status and position linked to a system always set apart from the one that orients the lives of the settled people around them, their projects set against the backdrop of a place but given meaning by a way of life that is not shared by the inhabitants of any single country.

Tameem's map is made of pieces of land that are his own but which are situated in the territories of several states. Their connections are not determined by the links among global cities, with their financial markets and cultural excitements, and their formation does not mimic the archipelago of holiday and fashion centers where the rich build pleasure palaces. His domain depends on states' laws, international agreements, and innumerable "expert systems." But in the end, it is defined by a bodily threshold, a corporal threshold of tolerance.

As I ponder this idea, I cannot help but be reminded of debates from the years when both Tameem and I lived in France. The last decade of the twentieth century was marked by the rapid politicization of immigration throughout Europe. In France, one of the debates that most intrigued me was the effort to determine a precise "*seuil de tolérance*," a threshold of tolerance, a measure of how much "strangeness" the social body could handle. What dose of immigrants could a neighborhood or a nation swallow and yet maintain its character? What measure of otherness might a society absorb without changing its mode of organization and endangering its institutional basis? One might interpret Tameem's mode of operation as setting a *seuil de tolérance* in terms of his own body rather than any body politic, turning the tables on anyone who imagines that his "problem" is one of seeking to be incorporated in a collectivity rooted in a common ground. Starting with his own displacements, he conceives a mode of operation that places himself and his bodily comfort at the center of the migration story. From asking how many people of diverse origins a neighborhood might take in without being itself transformed into a bit of foreign territory within a sovereign nation, we are left to wonder how long and how far the singular body might wander. Tolerance is no longer about measuring levels of foreignness or extending hospitality to travelers or migrants.[15] Its meaning is reduced and reconsidered in terms of a person plotting out resting points to construe the evolving background for his life. Will he reside in the places where he buys land? Will he circulate among the lands of his domain like a premodern monarch? His scheme does not include precise plans for the frequency of his visits. Nor does it include visions of the homes he might build or how he might dwell in them. But it does include a limit on the time spent in transit, a taking into account of the need to settle, if only to rest and then move on again. It seems a serial migrant like Tameem might entertain a romance with mobility, but one that projects his displacements against the map of the world at large; they are also inhabited by a pathos of bodily constraint.[16] One might be born with several passports in some forgotten place, rootless. But one must be born of someone; a body can move only from one place to another, and the horizon of anyone's potential destinations is limited by the unknown time of a lifespan.

For all the attention he pays to his "threshold of tolerance," Tameem's imaginative realm does not emerge from a seamless connection of moving body and intention in the manner of the nomad. Instead, it has evolved through opportunities to work with others. After studying architecture at Cooper Union, he owned a gallery with friends in New York. They lost a lot of money when a financial crisis hit, so they closed it. He moved to Paris to set up another gallery with his wife. After a few years, when that wasn't making any money either, he had an opportunity to get involved in building projects in Bahrain and decided to take it up.

Like many of the border-crossing people I met in the course of this research, Tameem declares that he has no trouble "feeling a part of wherever I live." Questions of assimilation or adaptation are simply not an issue for him; he is unfazed by the difficulties involved in becoming accustomed to new languages or customs. It is not in relation to some point of origin or some adopted way of life but through his "activity" with particular people and on specific projects that he feels "a part of things." He finds emotional sustenance and momentum in what he calls "social involvement" and collaborative activity. It is working toward a collective goal that he craves. It is the excitement of "getting involved" that keeps him motivated.

Collaboration is thus a key factor in determining his whereabouts at any point in time. But there are also places in all of his cities where he enjoys basking in a more diffuse social energy. While he has no roots, he has his "spots"—places where he meets friends and likes to just "hang out with people of all walks of life." The restaurant where I jotted down the conversations I relate here is one such gathering point. Located down the street from art galleries and a bookstore, the restaurant draws an international crowd along with well-heeled Bahrainis on weekdays.[17] But each weekend it is abandoned by these ex-pat managers in business attire and Bahrani ladies in their sequin-spangled robes when the neighborhood is invaded by packs of young Saudi men seeking to escape the strict controls imposed on public comportment in their country. They drive over the bridge that joins the Eastern Provinces to the island nation to indulge their desire for alcohol, clubbing, and sexual encounters, mirroring the trajectories of their richer cousins whose shopping sprees keep the couture houses of the Boulevard St. Honoré in business and prefiguring the Saudi youths who crossed the bridge in 2011, this time in military uniforms instead of the traditional *tob* or the latest brand of designer jeans.[18] The repression of the Bahrainis who were actors in the Arab Spring was terrible but not surprising. Bahrain has long been divided between those who voice the claims of a settled population, mainly Shi'a, and those who hold the power of the state thanks to family ties to the Arabian Peninsula, for whom a territory is like a plot of land that can be leased or worked by serfs, the state a family business with its projects and calculations, an inheritance that cannot be publicly traded.[19]

Indeed, even as Tameem enjoyed a leisurely lunch at the end of 2005, protests were already blocking the roads of the city to call attention to the inequitable treatment of the Shi'a majority by Sunni rulers with intimate ties to Saudi Arabia.[20] As we lingered over coffee on a weekday afternoon, Tameem invoked the difficulty he has had becoming engaged in political discussions. He emphasized that while he seeks out occasions for involvement with people wherever he goes, he "draws a line when it comes to talking about national politics." Although he holds UK and Bahraini passports, he doesn't "feel like a national anywhere." He recognizes that others might have national sentiments, but he himself simply doesn't experience that particular emotion. He does have strong feelings about political issues, but other people rarely agree with him; he says they find his ideas "nuanced or strange." Since he finds it difficult to communicate with others about political matters, he simply prefers to avoid them in conversation.

Nonetheless, a little later, when I began to tell him about my plans for travel over the subsequent months, he became unexpectedly emotional and animated. When I said that I would be traveling to Dubai the following week, he exclaimed, "I avoid Dubai like the plague!" My mention of Qatar set off a stream of comparisons: "Qatar and Kuwait are pretty much the same: that is, really bad." Bahrain is "not as bad as its wealthier neighbors," he explained, "but Saudi Arabia is the absolute worst." He has vowed that he will "never set foot in that kingdom." One might guess that someone who envisions his would-be dominion according to airline schedules would have strong feelings about different airports and the service on various carriers.[21] The fact that organizational procedures or timetables can evoke emotion and even loyalty has been documented by those who study bureaucracy.[22] But the strength of sentiment Tameem conveyed reveals something else. Might his reaction to setting foot on the land of particular countries offer a clue to comprehending his singular dream of buying up a personal space? Might it aid me in understanding exactly why "discussing national politics" is problematic for him in ways that it is not for other people? What he calls his "political gray zones" seem to result from his acute awareness of how states use not only their own territories but those of others in their strategies of region creation. The "strangeness" of his politics might be related to his avoidance of territories due to their being used as stages to elaborate particularly unappealing aspects of the regional theater of operations.[23]

Tameem's refusal to set foot in Saudi Arabia and his disdain of Dubai suggest that his sense of politics is "nuanced" because it evolves in a regional space that is difficult to articulate in terms of scales that move from the local to the global, national politics to international institutions.[24] His approach to politics is "strange" if one takes for granted the importance of the state for national politics and ignores the way states are caught up in a complex web of regional configurations. Experience has led him to conceive of politics in rapport with a territorial imagination that does not celebrate circulation or mobility but takes it as a given. His conceptions take notice of how various forms of striation can coexist and become entangled to shape projects. His own projects share a certain formal resemblance to these region-making strategies. He draws out his background in ways that recall archipelagos of military power, and highlights how he finds his motivation and *raison d'être* in collaboration with others. His mode of operation may not find easy expression in the political lexicon, but in practice, it is highly adapted to an environment where crossing into particular territories is often a way of avoiding conversations about the relationship of the body to the body politic and the state apparatus in the first place, where news is never about oneself or one's people, even when it purports to be produced for the entire world.

States increasingly see their territories as places of passage for populations in flux and increasingly work cooperatively to shape differentiated regional spaces to realize political projects of global import.[25] This is perhaps most apparent in regions like the Arab Gulf where family ties and family feuds are key elements of politics, where populations are ideally made of people who have been uprooted and can be moved to carry out defined projects for set periods of time. Tameem's unwillingness to cross borders is a sign of protest against the realization of a particular kind of project and confection of populations, as exemplified in Dubai. His refusal to step on Saudi soil is at once a reaction to the hypocrisy of a regime that directs impulses designated sinful toward other territories as a way to maintain its purity in keeping with a rigid interpretation of religious law, and something more. It is also a call to attend to how policies of circulation that "divide and conquer" by keeping people with those of their own ilk also have the potential to divide the citizen against himself. By making both Saudi Arabia and Dubai *haram* (forbidden) to him, by making both of them a no-man's-land on the map of his life, perhaps Tameem seeks to show the intimacy of the relationship between the two states. The difference in how they regulate who and what enters their territory and the kinds of activities that take place there is a performative ploy to detract attention from their complementarity and the mode of operation of a political subject that is both something more and something less than a state.

UNSETTLED STATES

States everywhere give access to their territories for particular intervals to specific kinds of people.[26] But the small states of the Persian Gulf are distinguished by how they compose their populations through migration, conceiving of their territories as places of temporary settlement. From the UAE to Abu Dhabi to Qatar, efforts to diversify the economy and attract a large palette of businesses have led to the expansion of sleepy coastal towns into major centers of population. The visible manifestations of each prince's imagination have taken the form of sprawling cities with daring skyscrapers and enormous malls. They are actions that symbolically demonstrate the competition among cousins that shapes the territory of the region according to lineage. Each state's population is composed mainly of people who are imported for set periods of time to carry out specific functions. A carefully calibrated system of immigration assures that most people's stay is provisional, with varied periods of residence allotted to people according to citizenship and the kinds of jobs they perform.

In the UAE or Qatar, a daily vision of the state's striating power is presented to residents and visitors alike. One sees uniform-wearing laborers from Kerala or Nepal being transported from their dormitories to factories or construction sites in old buses. Ex-pat Europeans, Americans, and some citizens of Arab countries live in walled compounds with swimming pools and have their own cars, sometimes with chauffeurs. Women from the Philippines work as maids and nannies, inhabiting single rooms in the homes of their employers. Although living conditions differ dramatically between the sometimes insalubrious quarters of the factory worker and the split-level five-bedroom homes of the managers, everyone is directed to associate with others of their kind. Access to the territory and international circulation follow the same logic of separation according to provenance and function. The hierarchy of people according to their origin and the kind of labor they carry out is clearly visible in the streets and serves to structure everyone's social life.[27] Nationals, who are a minority, have special privileges living among populations in perpetual circulation. Even those few immigrants who become citizens cannot truly become nationals; it is not in their blood.

In Saudi Arabia things are different. It is difficult for foreigners to enter the country or settle there. Pilgrims are of course welcome to visit the holy sites of Islam, but they are circulated according to their nationalities; like immigrant workers, they move as units and generally lodge together. A quota system controls the flow of people for the annual *haj*.[28] There is no need to dwell here on the strict prohibitions on the circulation of substances considered *haram* in the kingdom, or on women's circulation; these have been given ample attention in the international media. That "prayer police" enforce the obligation of prayer at regular intervals throughout the day is less often the object of media attention; but as elsewhere, the orientation of temporal rhythms is crucial to controlling citizens' movements and the "spots" where they might mix in ways that might threaten the regime's ordering principles.[29] To have a settled population is not always an advantage: it is much easier to "play" with and within territories if one's kingdom is populated by individuals whom one can bid to come or go at will.

Unlike their neighbors around the Gulf, the al-Saoud family rules a population made up of people who, like the rulers, tend to trace their ancestry to tribes that have called the Arabian Peninsula their home since time immemorial. But not all of these people are of the same bloodline.[30] Not everyone can trace their lineage to the prophet Mohammed or a venerable ancient tribe. Even among those who can, some have not prospered under the current dynasty. In addition to cleavages based on family rivalry, there are religious differences: one notes, for instance, the uneasy relationship between the state and its Shi'a minority. (We again recall the alacrity of the Saudi response to the Bahraini government's calls for help in repressing the thousands who peacefully demonstrated in 2011.) The legitimate claims of all settled citizens to the right to representation seems amply supported by international conventions and prevailing understandings of territorially based forms of government.[31] Yet these grounded people can be extremely problematic; not only are Saudi Shi'a settled in the regions richest in oil, but their religion is the majority creed in Iran, the Saudis' rival for regional hegemony. Keeping most Bahrainis "unsettled," making them strangers to their state, is a part of a broader, region-defining strategy that implicates states beyond the Gulf; one might recall the United States' support of the status quo during the Manama demonstrations of 2011.

Tameem can reside in Bahrain indefinitely. He is a citizen, yet he remains unsettled. "I am like the Indian migrant workers here," he says. "I am here to work and send money home to my family in Paris." He is joined to "his" country through his father's lineage, but with a smile that is only half ironic, he tells me that he is like a guest worker. What am I to make of this declaration? How can this educated, urbane man picture himself as similar to a guest worker, a common laborer, someone who washes the dishes? How dare he compare his comfortable situation to that of maids who care for other people's children while their own children are brought up by relatives in far-off countries? This last question leads me to a full stop in my internal conversation.

Although dire need cannot be the basis of his exile, Tameem lives far from his wife and child. Much as he refuses to enter Saudi Arabia, his wife and daughter refuse to live in the one place that offers him possibilities for business, because they cannot abide by the restrictions placed on women in Manama. If being a female European for hire on an immigrant visa is one thing, it is quite another to be the wife of someone deemed a "local." That would involve complex relationships with the extended family.[32] Thus, while Tameem's proclamation might be construed as demonstrating disregard for the hardship of those who move with difficulty and labor tirelessly to support extended families who live in poverty, my internal debate leads me to think it might be important to pay closer attention to the direction in which his emotions as well as his profits flow.

I cannot be sure, but I imagine that in drawing attention to his "migration" to the strange country that is on paper his own, he conveys what he must feel to be the invisibility of the uncanny nature of his belonging to the place he lives but will not settle. What does it mean to be "of" a place that is so easily turned into a space for the powerful neighbor to discharge its illicit urges? To be in some way related to the powerful who disengage themselves from the idea that settlement should be a gauge of political legitimacy? What would it be like to live among those who are willing to turn the territory of a state into an empty quarter of the soul to preserve territories deemed sacred from the unruly desires of the people who inhabit them? In a world in flux, maps remain intact; some places are harder to settle than others and even those engaged in regional Realpolitik make ironic use of borders.

To explore how choreographies of power are related to the backgrounds against which individual faces and lives might be projected does not mean discarding paradigms of settling. Rather, it involves moving away from an emphasis on oppositions of stasis to mobility and instead seeking to understand when and why certain backgrounds come to the fore and how particular ways of moving encourage manners of settling down and making oneself at home.

IMMIGRATION AS A HOMELAND

Alice lives in Paris, but she was not born there. Tracing her origins is not easy. Her great-great-grandmother Marie Elise Richter, originally from Luxembourg, moved to Paris as a young married woman. She gave birth to Alice's great-grandmother in Paris, but the young girl was sent to school in Luxembourg. She was not a brilliant student and ended up studying millinery in London, where she fell in love with a Brazilian. When World War I began, she was pregnant with their child. He returned to Brazil, but she refused to accompany him. The child—Alice's grandmother Jacqueline Bernard—was thus born in London and lived there for a few years. During this time, her mother—Alice's great-grandmother—had a long relationship with Gottardo Lavarello, an Italian. "It was a free union right out of the belle époque," Alice explains. Their love did not last, however, and after a few years Alice's great-grandmother left Lavarello for an Italian count and then in 1938 "or thereabout" she married Marcel Richard and moved to Paris. Jacqueline remained attached to Lavarello and decided to live with him in Italy. She later married Carlo Marcoli, an Italian from Genoa. It was her grandmother Jacqueline's house in Genoa that Alice called home for many years. Alice's mother is Italian.

And this is only the story of one side of Alice's family—her mother's. Her father, Enrique, was from Venezuela. It was only when Enrique was posted as a diplomat in British Guyana that Alice really got to know her Venezuelan family.

Alice grew up all around the world, and although she remembers her grandmother's house in Italy as a kind of base, she can point to no particular place of origin. She grew up in a close-knit family of three, moving across the background of the world. It was only when she moved to New York at eighteen that she found "her place." There she was able to draw on narratives of journeying to a new homeland to knit herself into a city that is defined by its entanglement in migration. Her journey there was not marked by a painful uprooting; indeed, one could interpret it as a flight from a background that was at once too much defined by particular individuals—her parents, who had an extremely close relationship—set against the background of the entire globe. Alice's experiences as a child provided her with some of the skills and flexibilities of serial migrants with a more conventional migration story. She spoke several languages fluently from an early age and was fortunate to have received an elite education. But in certain ways the very complexity of her family story and her capacity to adjust to circumstances made her attachment to the story of migration and the social fabric it weaves in New York especially strong. What other discourse of belonging might pull her in? What other socially meaningful line might she hang on to? New York's way of defining itself as a gateway for immigrants allowed Alice to settle and feel at home. In a city where so many residents are foreign-born, Alice's lack of a defined place of origin was not remarkable. Being labeled an immigrant hides important truths about stories of serial migration; her association with immigration in New York was noteworthy in that it was through immigration that she found a point of attachment, a place from which to move on.

Alice first spent time in Paris in 1984 on a "year abroad" program. She returned again in 1992 to conduct research on immigration and incarceration in France for her doctoral dissertation at Columbia University. It was while carrying out this research that she met and fell in love with the man who would become the father of her children, an ex-con and activist in the *beur* movement in France—"*beur*" is a slang word that inverts "*arabe*"—named Mohamed Hocine.[33] Although her relationship with him did not last, she remained in Paris to raise her children. To a certain extent France felt to her like an extension of her grandmother's house in Italy or the apartment she and her family kept in Rome and where they lived on and off between her father's assignments. Alice says that it took her many years to leave behind the idea that she was a New Yorker. Although she has always been comfortable in Paris because it "feels European," it is only since she bought an apartment of her own that she has started to feel settled.

Like the father of her children, the man who has been Alice's partner for many years was born in France but is perceived as an "immigrant" because he is of Algerian origin. Her children are also perceived as "immigrants" and "Arabs." In point of fact, however, Alice is the only immigrant in the family. Her children tease her about it, calling her a *bledard*, a pejorative term that comes from the Arabic word for the countryside (*bled*)—someone "just off the boat," as one might say in the United States. Which *bled* she is from is not important; the point is that she arrived in Paris from somewhere else. The challenges they face as *beurs* are not easy for them to articulate except in contrast to their mother's freedom of motion, her ease at moving through a city that views them as problematic. They are the ones who are often asked to show their identity papers to the police when they take the metro. Unlike parents who are anxious about the gang their children hang out with, the drugs they might try, or the kinds of mischief they might get into, Alice says that her main concern is that her boys might be unjustly held by the "forces of order."[34] They were born into a breach of French history that makes Alice a stranger to the world they inhabit. They find themselves caught between two spaces of the imagination, but with a single place of reference.

Alice hopes to be able to help her sons travel more as they get older. She thinks that an experience of actually living in other places is valuable. But what might be the nature of this experience she values and wants to share with them? She herself says she fears feeling too settled. Is it not best to at least imagine that one might keep things open? Admit the possibility of living somewhere else? She remarks that her partner "has never even taken a plane," and yet he has broad ideas about the world. Alice's choice to carry out research on immigration and incarceration in France could be seen as a sign that she takes a cosmopolitan interest in the "other"; what could be more different from her experience than someone marked as from a particular country or ethnic group and confined to a cell? What could be less like her experience of feeling a home through immigration in New York than the experience of growing up with a single homeland yet perceived as a potential criminal because one is an "immigrant"? A number of those seeking to develop a cosmopolitan ethos have singled out immigrants, exiles, and refugees as requiring particular attention and support. It is with these displaced people in mind that Jacques Derrida, for one, has suggested that Europe needs to conceive new forms of hospitality.[35] Yet to understand Alice's engagement with the relationship of imaginative to geographic mobility in terms of hospitality for others would belittle the intensity and depth of her engagement with immigration as a source of herself.

All serial migrants move through immigration and then repeat the experience. Unlike the nomad, they rely on essential conceptions of culture or nationality or social position to punctuate their life narratives. They do not ignore borders but turn standard maps of the world into the grounds upon which to unfold themselves, taking possession of each new country by making it into a chapter of their lives. When they contrast their experiences in the places that form the intervals of their lives, or when they work on themselves by living through different social positions in their various homes, serial migrants do not eschew settled notions of positioning and incorporation like Simmel's individuals. Indeed, they rely on them. At a time when some states maintain military archipelagos across the globe and others constitute their populations with people constrained to circulate among countries at regular intervals, the nomad as figured by the philosophers is a contemporary Don Quixote, his windmills the settled and settling states of a fading political imagination. To follow the flow of Tameem's emotions and embrace the intensity of Alice's engagement with immigration, one needs to pay closer attention to how specific paths generate distinctly different kinds of subjects, each with its unique way of participating in a political dance that involves nomadic states and wanderers whose modes of operations are state-like, or state-inspired. Serial migrants are not made of many places but of a shared experience: they have all moved out of immigration.

CHAPTER 3

MOVING THROUGH
IMMIGRATION

IMMIGRANTS LIVE BETWEEN. Their displacements are set between two countries, two ways of life. Their stories progress through either/or propositions, alternating presence and absence, here to there. Economists explain these movements in terms of market pushes and pulls. Novelists tell tales of how two social and cultural worlds correlate, collide, or commingle in immigrant life[1] Political pundits thrive on debates about migration's impact and the immigrant's image. When immigrant stories are sewn into the very fabric of the nation's tales, the perils and rewards of these journeys are woven into the collective narrative.[2] When they are not, and when the unidirectional nature of the immigrant's pathways becomes apparent, immigration begins to be perceived as problematic.[3]

The flood of words and pictures produced in the process of explaining migration often mimics the stories that history tells. Waves of population are said to periodically wash over the world. Metaphors of flooding and flow are adopted to mimic migratory processes.[4] But there is little fluidity in the immigrant experience. Some people feel threatened by the countless directions from which immigrants arrive;

others are upset that the immigrant might set up her home among them, altering their relationships to their neighbors. This often makes the immigrant a subject of politics that tends to obscure the fact that the defining dynamic of immigration is highly regular. With or without official documents and regardless of place of origin or profession, immigrants are settled into continual moves between home and host countries.

It is through a movement from the place of birth to the land of another state that the immigrant's status is determined. Contrasts of "here" to "there" are at the center of immigration from the moment someone takes off on this once-in-a-lifetime journey. The immigrant is never settled within himself; his very being is divided; the effort to find balance between two homes preoccupies him. Because widespread understandings about how bodies and persons are produced assume that a person becomes herself within a single national and cultural milieu or context, the immigrant is an intrinsically problematic figure. On one hand, she might appear inauthentic or untrue to those she leaves behind because she adopts new ways of life when she changes environments. On the other, her body might appear to be a piece of foreign territory or an exemplar of "her" culture, a provocative challenge to prevailing conceptions of civilization in her new homeland.[5]

Recent research has shown that by taking into account the two poles that orient immigrant life—"here" and "there"—we might draw a more accurate picture of how migration is changing with globalization.[6] Both "sending" and "receiving" states derive economic benefit from immigrants and absent nationals. These in-between people enable both their homelands to consolidate national, ethnic classifications, which are used as the basis for studying how immigrants forge transnational ties. These meetings of strangers with their new homelands may be rife with imaginative possibilities because the process gives birth to a third space of imaginative hybridization. Yet even this space of the imagination evolves within the confines of the polarity that is immigration's defining feature. A third space thus conceived might allow someone to work or live creatively, but it cannot extract her from the swaying of the immigration pendulum.

Whether migration is carefully planned for years or undertaken suddenly in the dead of night, departures from one's place of origin and arrivals in a strange, new environment characterize the immigrant experience. In literature and film, public opinion, or scholarly debates, the move from one country to another is depicted as a singular, often difficult rite of passage. But what happens if the immigrant moves on, if the immigrant story is repeated?

OTHER IMMIGRANTS

Ela explained that she knew from the age of eight that she would leave Romania. At eighteen she moved to the United States and married. She divorced her American husband after a couple of years and moved to Paris, where she attended American University. She then lived in New York for a while before setting off for Uzbekistan, where she worked as a journalist for *Forbes*. She traveled briefly to Sri Lanka for another job before settling in Bahrain in order to be close to her boyfriend, who works in Saudi Arabia.[7] When I met her in Manama, she had been employed by a Bahraini government agency for several years.

As we enjoyed a coffee on the terrace of a pleasant café, we gossiped about people we both knew in Paris before going on to discuss how having several homelands makes one feel different from people who have stayed where they were born. But in attempting to develop a more precise idea of what characterizes lives of serial migration, Ela did not dwell on oppositions of mobility to settlement but instead told the story of her life in contrast to that of her brother, whom she described as a "regular immigrant." She told me, "He lives in Germany with his wife and child and does the usual immigrant thing. He works in a factory and is not really integrating in Germany, just lives there to make money, and returns home for vacation every summer." In her estimation, his move was "purely for economic reasons," implying through comparison that her own journeys have been undertaken for other motives. She emphasizes that the disparity in their conditions, motivations, and lifestyles could hardly be greater and explains this gap as the result of a life project she has envisioned from the time she was a child. From the very beginning, it seems, she was just a different type of person.

Unlike the immigrant, Ela seems to have managed to subordinate the world map to her personal objectives. When she projects herself against the immigrant's image, her own ability to travel unimpeded in a variety of directions is highlighted. One gets the impression that she never really passed through a stage of immigration; she had it all planned from the beginning. Perhaps even her marriage in America was part of a plan to acquire a passport that would enable her to travel freely. Is she a new kind of displaced person, detached from any territorial or cultural mooring, having earned her place as a member of a new professional class?[8] Ela does not give herself a label; she is too much of an individualist for that! But the kind of typological distinction she makes between herself and the immigrant is intriguing because of its similarity to the categorizations and definitions of different migratory trajectories in academic discussions. Immigrants, global nomads, cosmopolitans, travelers, members of the international managerial class—the image of each is fleeting but serves to distinguish people on the move in terms of economic, social, and personal characteristics.[9]

Bashir also distinguishes himself from other immigrants. He fled the civil war in Lebanon to live in the United States in the 1980s. He worked as a hairdresser in the Midwest for several years, hoping to obtain immigration papers and eventually a green card, but he was unsuccessful. In the early 1990s he jumped at the opportunity to work in the UAE.

When we met in 2005, he was working in a salon in Dubai. Business was pretty good. "I regretted not being able to settle in America, but when things are not going well around you, you have to be always ready to move on," he explained. In Lebanon there was the war, and even at the time of our meeting, he said that things there were not stable, so he had no dreams of returning. He presciently observed that the situation in Dubai was also uncertain, "too artificial to last."[10] And so, he told me, he is always entertaining ideas about where he might settle next. Should there be an attack or a financial crash, he has to keep his options open. His avid reading of newspapers and blogs in Arabic and English leads him to envisage other places he might live, countries he might consider for his next displacement. Australia? Venezuela? He feels that he needs to stay focused on being able to move on "when things in Dubai get bad."

Expressing no desire to live somewhere in particular, Bashir has no zest for travel and no long-term plans. Instead, his experience makes him question the very solidity and stability of place that many people take for granted. His lively interest in world affairs is not a theoretical endeavor but an effort to keep ahead of political and economic crises. Mobility is not a grand project but a matter of survival. The immigrant he imagines is someone who has been lucky enough to settle in a place where there was little turmoil or uncertainty. He envies those who are not forever on the lookout for possible future homelands.

While Ela might be imagined as a chameleon of global capitalism, lacking a sense of the values that make for community and loyalty and relentless in her pursuit of personal development, Bashir could be portrayed as a victim of the world system. Still, they have more in common than such characterizations would suggest. They differ in their conceptions of a "typical immigrant," but they both develop their own stories in contrast to that immigrant's situation. Bashir may regret that the US administration did not allow him to settle, but like Ela, he now conceives of his life as being somehow outside immigration, beyond the shifts between home and host countries. Tameem's apparent class-blindness comes to mind; his comparison of himself with the guest worker contrasts with Alice's sense that her complex entanglement with immigration shows her difference from the immigrant. For all the disparities among these people, there is something about immigration that brings them closer: they share a sense of being misrecognized in relation to the immigrant. It may come from being labeled as immigrants where they currently reside, or it may be due to their own unwillingness to see the similarity between their lives and those of "other immigrants." In both cases their migratory path is obscured or assumed to be of little importance.

Setting lives of serial migrants against the mental displacement of the cosmopolitan and the nomad's active opposition to settled orders has brought us to the similarity of the underlying rhythms that shape these figures. Presenting salient aspects of the experience of particular serial migrants has enabled me to counter the abstraction of the cosmopolitan or the nomad's Manichaeism and suggest that unequal access to forms of settlement is important for self-consolidation of individuals and states alike. But it is only by reference to the immigrant that an idea of the common experience of serial migrants begins to take form. It is once one notices that all serial migrants have moved through immigration, and that this experience has generally gone unrecognized, that this distinct form of life with its particular pathologies and modes of self-problematization can be examined.

Ela seeks to distance herself from her brother's situation as a "regular migrant" at all costs, and most serial migrants do not engage with immigration in its multiplicity as deeply as Alice does. But the fact that many of them explain their efforts to aid or teach "first-time immigrants" is integral to the picture of how immigration has shaped their self-understanding. Leila volunteers as a translator for an association that helps immigrants from North Africa in Montreal. Although it is not always easy to encounter fellow Indians in Qatar, because his executive position means that he lives in a compound far from laborers' quarters, Akhil, who holds an advanced degree from an American university, says that he makes a point of "helping out" laborers from India with their paperwork or practical problems. He remarks that his discussions with them often follow the same rhythms and traverse the same topics as those with his American wife, who is also a "first-time immigrant." Like Akhil, she is educated and lives what he calls a "comfortable, middle-class lifestyle," but his experience of leaving India to live in Britain and then moving to the United States for graduate school and then to work makes him as serial migrant. Gaps in education or status, the way people are variously identified by race, nationality, or citizenship in their diverse homelands, are far from inconsequential, but as Tameem's sketch of himself as a guest worker suggests, to concentrate primarily on these criteria is to ignore how migrants' similar trajectories shape their lives.

Anissa emphasizes that migration can be done gracefully; immigration involves skill. When her family left their comfortable home in Rabat for a new life in Montreal, it was "a kind of balancing act to move the family." She was able to "handle it" because she had already gained experience when she moved on her own from Tangiers to France, then back to Morocco with her husband. She says that she had become practiced at preparing her travel and envisioning her upcoming settlement. This was what made her different from "other immigrants," those who moved for "the first time." With each displacement she had learned how to move not only more efficiently but "better"; she now feels more composed, more in control of both her practical affairs and her affect. She has acquired a certain balance, a certain confidence that the complex processes involved in displacement will go smoothly, a sense of how to move with grace that extends into her way of relating to others in her new place of residence. Of course, tickets must be purchased, passports and visas must be in order; one conducts research into possibilities for employment and schools for the children. One takes an inventory of one's possessions to decide what to take along and checks out possibilities for housing.[11] But there is also a process of projecting oneself into an unknown place that draws on gestures and knowledge and confidence acquired through what one has accomplished in the past. The experience of a first migration is important in gaining the confidence to move a second time.

When my research assistant Elizabeth interviewed Fiona in London, they discussed how difficult the first migration can be even for those who never plan to settle into the new homeland forever. Fiona described how it took her time to adjust when she moved from New Zealand to Japan. She told Elizabeth that "dealing with spiders was a problem":

> E: Oh, are there a lot of spiders?
>
> F: Yes, there was a gap in my door and the spiders were huge. They like them because in Japan they think that [the spiders] will eat the cockroaches, but in New Zealand we do not have such spiders. I could not sleep. I was terrified and I would cry.
>
> E: So you prefer the cockroaches?
>
> F: I still had cockroaches.
>
> E: Do they bite people?
>
> F: No, they are just big and they run really fast. I had one as big as my hand. They can flatten themselves and you knew that they could get in anywhere. One came under my door and it went into the cupboard with my bedding and I was just crying. My friend looked everywhere and could not find them. My first year they came out of the plughole in the shower. I killed one on the wall with a flyswatter and it fell in my hair. Then I got more and more brave and the second year I did not see any. It was really interesting. The second year I did not have a problem; I guess I had gotten brave and they did not want to bother me anymore.

Crossing a border, even with the best of passports, can be daunting. It takes time to learn a way of life, to conquer the fear of being overwhelmed by strange creatures while one is exposed, naked, and wet. People who attempt a second migration are often those who have

managed to come to terms with the challenges of settlement, those
for whom a memory of their perseverance in fitting into the new
environment has taken shape. They, like Fiona, have found a way of
"becoming brave."

Abderahman's account of the challenges of working with "first-time
immigrants" to produce pan-Arab television in Dubai offers insight
into the difference between a first migration and a later one, in terms
of both the migration itself and the relationship the repeat migrant has
to "first-timers." Abderahman was born and raised in Saudi Arabia,
then moved to the United States, where he earned a master's degree
in journalism at American University in Washington D.C. After
graduation he stayed on in the United States to work as a journalist.
Then a few years later he was hired by a pan-Arab newspaper based
in London, and during his years in the UK he became a well-known
figure in the Arab media.[12] He moved to Dubai to become the director
of news at Al Arabiya television. When I visited the newsroom in late
2005, he was directing a team of people from thirty-four countries to
produce the programming for the channel, which was started with
Saudi investors. They compete for viewers with Al Jazeera, based in
Qatar, as well as a host of other pan-Arab channels.

That "local knowledge" on a news item is best gathered and
conveyed by people who seem to be "of" a place is a widely accepted
idea. However, Abderahman emphasizes that each local viewpoint is
always limited. The work habits of the journalists and technicians
brought together in his newsroom were developed mainly in contexts
where media are in the service of the ruling regime or royal families.
A "grounded" perspective thus includes partial or biased reporting. A
certain slant on issues is also apparent in Arab media because some
nationalities, like Egyptians and Lebanese, are more numerous than
others, like Sudanese or Algerians. But generally, he contends, the
gathering of people from different countries to produce news leads to
a balancing of perspectives and well-rounded stories; one might say

that the different objects of avoidance or attraction among the various national viewpoints cancel one another out. This is in line with the idea that national diversity in the workplace leads to creativity and a broader perspective, an idea advanced by scholars, business leaders, and policymakers who argue for increased and easier migration for educated people everywhere.[13]

One might be tempted to envision this Dubai newsroom as a scene for Habermasian ideal conversations about world issues and a place to explore how a disparate group of people might undergo a process of cosmopolitanization together. In this case, however, the leap from national to worldly consciousness is made in the context of an organization dedicated to reshaping the Arab World before taking on the task of providing news to the entire world. Abderahman recognizes that the region-building nature of his project affects the extent of what he can accomplish. He maintains that his experience of serial migration helps him to manage this complex environment.

It was in Washington that he developed his ideals about journalism and the accent he still carries with him when speaking English. As a young man he adapted to a way of life that was extremely different from what he had known in his homeland. When he moved from the United States to England, he saw that although immigration had broadened his perspectives, it had also led him to generalize about the world in terms of contrasts between his two places. While living in Washington, he had made constant comparisons of Saudi Arabia and America. He tended to perceive "the West" in terms of what he knew of America, just as his experience of the entire Arab and Muslim world came from his childhood in Saudi Arabia. Living in London for many years, and then moving to Dubai, gave him a more nuanced sense of things; he feels that the experience of settling in several countries has made him "more precise and clearer-headed." It has helped him to develop a more "personal perspective" and to give voice to it, something that other people do not always appreciate. Indeed, although Abderahman's involvement in the region-building work taking place in the Gulf is quite different from Tameem's, and although his tone is more gleefully ironic, he too explains that he is often misunderstood, the "oddness" of his views simply written off as "American."

He says that his peregrinations have given him a "sense of humor" when people tease him about seeming "too American." Yet it is his Saudi nationality that has allowed him to hold key positions, to be a player in the top levels of an evolving geopolitical landscape. The Arab world as produced in his newsroom is perhaps as real as any other: the regional audiences his journalists imagine based on their limited experience, those East/West dichotomies he encourages them to explore by interacting with each other, are often conceived in ways that are not so different from the "othering" processes Edward Said drew attention to several decades ago in his *Orientalism*. Abderahman himself notes that his strong and ongoing ties to the United States do make him seem "less Arab," but one must wonder if this is because of a simple equation of his political line with that of Washington, or to the indelible mark a first migration seems to leave on serial migrants. Maybe his colleagues simply have no terms to express what they might perceive as his "strangeness." Perhaps he is able to laugh off these comments, because in such remarks, as in so many other things, he recognizes himself at an earlier stage of his life. "First-time migrants think about the world in terms of two alternatives," he says. "They generalize about whole regions based on very limited experiences." Given that in Dubai it is difficult to gain a sense of settling into anything but one's work milieu, Abderahman himself helps to shape the Arab world by framing the life-world of his "first-time immigrant" journalists, challenging their ideas about their own experience of migration and their judgments of what it means to belong.

AFTER IMMIGRATION

Although serial migrants may distinguish themselves from those who migrate for the first time, they are themselves often taken for immigrants, *tout court*. They have trouble expressing why or how their experiences are similar, even though many of them are excited to learn that I'm trying to understand what makes us different. Although I convened several assemblies in universities and coffee shops in the course of this project, serial migrants do not spontaneously assemble. The singular experience they share is independent of the places they have lived or the places they might meet; it does not correspond to a position or status or style. It is the repetition of the experience of migration that they hold in common; each of them can tell a story of stepping beyond the first immigration.

When someone ventures beyond the endpoint of immigration, she shifts from a narrative in which she is pulled between two places, peoples, and cultures toward a situation in which the primacy of place, the warm embrace of community, and the received ideas of culture are subordinated to her life story.[14] Whether the logical infinity of further homelands is celebrated or accepted with resignation is irrelevant to what produces this subject in all of its generality. One moves from a fixation on the questions of contextualization to which the immigrant is subjected toward a definition of place in terms of the times of a life. In the tow of my subjects through repeated immigration, I come to see that it is not some general propensity for mobility that they share. From concerns of the way the immigrant might be integrated, assimilated, or rejected by a settled society, my attention is turned to the way countries become intervals in the evolving narrative of an individual's life.

As I reread, recall, and follow the life stories of people who shared with me the stories of their lives across several countries, I find that they show little concern with the problems that shape others' ideas about immigration—"feeling at home" or "integrating" or "assimilating." Instead, they worry about a place becoming "impossible" because of political or economic circumstances. They fret about feeling "stuck" in any one place, for they seem to take it as a sign of a more general foreclosure of life's possibilities. These possibilities obviously differ for each of them. We might be impatient to delve into how differences of birthplace, education, or wealth determine the way serial migrants arrange life's intervals. But while it is tempting to examine what distinguishes the different paths of those who have repeated the migration story, jumping too hastily in this direction would keep us from noticing what they have in common. Our encounter with the nomad has led us to observe that those who migrate cannot dispute or ignore states' borders; indeed, they are the migrant's obsession. But it is now time to clarify how serial migrants turn frontiers into events, countries into chapters in their life stories.

People with several homelands invariably begin their life stories by relating their progression through periods of time that they label with the names of the countries they have lived in. Initially, they tell a story of straightforward progress, recounting each move from one home to another according to how it led them to where they are at present, threading places like pearls onto the string that is their lifeline. A common manner of working with intervals defined by border crossings constitutes each serial migrant's experience. This does not mean that those from a particular place or those who have settled in the same places or speak the same languages share nothing in particular.[15] Nor does it imply that serial migrants have nothing in common with neighbors who have never moved at all. What it does suggest, however, is that the reiteration of migration leads to particular possibilities for using political and cultural units to shape oneself. By arranging their life narratives in terms of periods defined by political territories, serial migrants share a framework for imagining who they are and the subjects they are or might become. Commonality is thus made of forms for problematizing the self rather than by occupying a similar position in a settled social structure or unconsciously transmitted culture.

One might read stories of serial migration in terms of Hayden White's discussion of "emplotment." He writes:

> The kind of interpretation typically produced by the historical discourse is that which endows what would otherwise remain only chronologically ordered series of events with the formal coherency of the kind of plot structure met with in narrative fiction. This endowment of a chronicle of events with a plot structure, which I call the operation of emplotment, is carried out by discursive techniques that are more often tropological than logical in nature.[16]

White sees the codes that order events into specific temporal units as culturally specific, whereas narratives of serial migration show regularities in form and tropological possibilities that cut across the way these individuals might be associated with some cultural origin or shared trajectory. His recognition that there are competing ways of emplotting a narrative is suggestive in terms of how and why serial migrants' stories are assimilated to the immigrant's story.[17]

Turning homelands into periods of lives leads to a subordination of place to time. A life of migration centers attention on moves from one place to another; a territory appears as a time period in a longer story. A serial migrant often does project her image against first one and then another settled background. Indeed, she might derive self-knowledge and give her story momentum through the process of submitting herself to different regimes and observing how she is variously positioned and labeled in different places. She might note the differences of terrain, the different coping skills required in each place. But the serial migrant always stitches together the places and times of life by repeating the immigrant's defining journey. It is not only by moving through and beyond a situation of immigration but also by reiterating immigration's *pas de bourrée* that serial migrants move their lives forward across borders. The repetition of the migration journey creates a dynamic dialectic, one that progresses by spinning a thread between the place one is now and the next destination. Jorge says:

> When I get ready to move in a new place, I remember my previous departures, recall the preparations, the feelings I had. I think of how I never imagined having so many places in my life. I remember certain details of life in each place and what it was like leaving behind friends, a job, and a home. I recall what it was like to arrive in the place I am now leaving. I remember the turn of the key in the previous door as I lock the one I leave now. I close my eyes and recall the homes I lived in, the faces of my friends and how people in each place say my name.

One lives in one place first, then moves to a second or third. While each country appears as an interval in a longer story without a definitive endpoint, scenes of departure remain focused on a particular move between two points of settlement. With each move, what is supposed to be a once-in-a-lifetime journey is reenacted.[18] Departure is a time when life's threads are undone, its pearl-like intervals rearranged in new or unlikely combinations. As practical preparations progress, memories of previous leave-takings animate one's actions just as previous intervals of life shape the present. One seeks to weave the future homeland into the present, rearranging the position and meaning of each homeland in the series.[19]

If the journey from one's place of birth to a second country defines the immigrant, the repetition of the journey might be likened to a ritual. Rites of passage and rituals are set off from the ordinary by particular gestures, trips, or incantations; they may involve designated places or movements over a particular terrain. They remove the individual or the group from everyday time and relationships and suspend habitual modes of ideation. But rites of passage involve a singular alteration of a person's status, while rituals can be repeated.[20] Rites of passage present the collectivity as witness to the changes in an individual or group, whereas ritual acts on the community as a whole. Even seemingly individual rituals, such as personal prayers, are assumed to be effective because they invoke a shared God and engage a system of belief shared by others.[21] While these rituals do not necessarily involve the actual presence of a group, they associate ritual efficacy with a consciously shared set of actions, a foundational text, or an imagined community. In fact, ritual actions conducted without such a communal setting are perceived as signs of neurosis or superstition. It is precisely this lack of collective recognition that characterizes the situation of the person who, after living as an immigrant in a second country, moves on to a third. In the eyes of the law, the census, and those around him, he has not changed; he is still an immigrant. His repetition of the immigration story goes unnoticed.[22]

Rites of passage are made up of three stages, according to Arnold Van Gennep: first, a time of separation from the everyday; second, a period of transformation and transition during which the individual is untied from society and ordinary time; and third, a period of reintegration of the person into day-to-day life in a new position. While the rite of passage is, for the individual, a once-in-a-lifetime affair, its repetition is a key element of social reproduction. Individuals change status, but the roles remain stable. Something rather different happens, however, when one adapts this model to understand a rite that is recognized worldwide but then fails to notice that its repetition causes it to take on certain ritual-like qualities for the individual. In response to those who interpreted the repetitive movements of ritual as an outlet for societal tensions or as an occasion when the basic structures and relationships of a group are represented and reconfirmed, Victor Turner developed Van Gennep's observations to conceive rituals as imaginative, inspired happenings. The reiteration of particular words or gestures leads to a liminal time when thoughts and emotions mingle freely. At the height of the experience of in-between moments, the community engulfs itself in a heady brew of flowing culture that leads to changes in the very structure of the collectivity. "It is the analysis of culture into factors and their free recombination in any and every possible pattern, however weird, that is most characteristic of liminality," Turner asserts.[23] It is the experience of *communitas* that enables creative transformation.

Unlike the novice's transformation or the immigrant's passage, ritual is conceived as a collective experience. What matters is not just the reference to some social entity or shared deity, but the actual experience of community. Everyone, it seems, can be expected to seek out situations in which fellow feeling is expressed and leads to social transformations—even those who as outsiders to the community of reference occupy "betwixt and between" positions. According to Turner, for mid-twentieth-century America those outsiders

> would include migrant foreigners, second generation Americans, persons of mixed ethnic origin, parvenus (upwardly mobile marginals), migrants from country to city, and women in a changed, nontraditional role. What is interesting about such marginals is that they often look to their group of origin, the so-called inferior group, for communitas, and to the more prestigious group in which they mainly live and in which they aspire to higher status as their structural reference group.[24]

It is easy to dismiss Turner's assumptions about the status of immigrants because his notions about tradition in America are dated. Don't we now study transnational networks, diasporas, and the way that those caught between two worlds participate in shaping the cultural and political reference points we take for granted? Indeed, the way we relate to marginality has shifted. Critiques of culture, calls for a mobile sociology, and theories of globalization lead people to question the self-evident makeup of culture and society and community. Yet for many activists and politicians and scholars, dreams of *communitas* continue to inspire the outlines of action and study. Even as scholars increasingly take into account the variety of movements of people across borders, associations between individuals and their places and cultures of origin continue to inform our ideas about how mobility can be relevant to politics and culture. But when what is conceived as a singular journey begins to become something of a habit, when the liminal temporality of the border crossing becomes a regularly practiced skill, when each homeland becomes one in a set that make up a life, it becomes difficult to sort out the vast array of cultural elements that might be accumulated in the migrant's journey or to find the source of his foreignness. Which homeland might the serial migrant represent? Which culture might she call on to transform which community? By conceiving of the immigration story as a rite of passage to which the world at large bears witness, we enter into a series of investigations into how dissimilar modes of movement define particular forms of life and subjectivity.

Interpreting the immigration journey as a ritual leads me to leave behind ideas of the serial migrant as either simply another immigrant or a footloose free spirit. Drawing on Turner's insights on structural rearrangements in liminal states, we notice how reiteration of the scene of moving homelands leads one to enter a distinct temporality. People describe intense recollections in the elastic time between departure and arrival. They speak of life-reassessments and bringing the places of the past into the present. But unlike the collective rituals Turner exalts as transformative, the cultural references and practices even for a single individual are often diverse and potentially confusing. One might travel with family and friends, but to add their reference points to conceive a hybrid, collective subject leads away from any singular, shared point of reference, let alone to a *communitas* that would transform any collective structures. The moments between departure and arrival do not involve a free, creative mingling of symbols but instead highlight the way that bordered territories mark the times of an evolving life story. Even as they make the passage between one home and a new one, serial migrants' stories are not as malleable and mixable or fragmented as one might imagine, nor are the images of the places they move through stable enough to serve as backgrounds one might blend into or shine against. Is it simply that the vessel of the self is too fragile to hold the currents of the many cultural streams of several homelands?

To move and then to move again does not lead the serial migrant out of immigration's double bind. Instead, the repetition of the migration story amplifies, confuses, augments, and renders more apparent the bipolarity of the immigrant experience. No matter how many homelands might be added to one's story, each displacement establishes relationships among two states, two territories, tying together two places at the same time as the entire narrative is refashioned. The addition of a third country introduces prospects for remaking the relationship of the prior two homelands; the introduction of a third term provokes new possibilities for representing the original two. In contrast to the immigrant who might compare her singular displacement to the second country with the displacements of others who have made a move in a similar direction, repeated departures lead serial migrants to confront themselves as they appear in distinct places at different times.

Crossing territories marked by the map allows an evolving framing of oneself over time, encouraging a process of self-mimesis. One might remark that such confrontations of life's moments and places occur in everyone's self-reflections. While this is true, the parallels between serial migrants' intervals and the borders that make up the maps of world politics open up a particularly instructive set of questions about such self-to-self reflections. Serial migrants' life stories involve many of the same continuities and changes as those of people who never move at all, but their various countries act as signposts, offering them particular kinds of resources in establishing relationships among different versions of themselves, or modes of evaluating themselves. It is by reference to how each different country involves different configurations of life's continuities that they explain their stories. The time between each departure and arrival is an occasion to reinterpret the place of each of life's intervals. It is not simply about moving forward with some lifelong abstract project, weaving more threads into the existing lifeline, but an opportunity to find new ways of weaving the places and times of life together.

Pierre Bourdieu writes that "time is indeed, as Kant maintained, the product of an act of construction, but it is the work not of the thinking consciousness but of the dispositions and practices."[25] Anissa concurs that practice is essential to the work of time, but it is precisely in the evolution of her own dispositions that her moves make apparent that repeating similar movements can produce awareness of how practice shapes consciousness. Each migration initiates a process that works on the relationship of the present to the future in ways that cannot easily be reconciled with notions of personal background that are premised on the unconscious acquisition of the taken-for-granted gestures. Serial migration may encourage the subject to let go of certain habits, not just take her distance from inherited dispositions. It also allows her to put herself in situations in which she develops new tastes and skills in ways that may surprise her but which involve some measure of conscious deliberation. She tests herself as she seems to be at present against a new background, but also opens up new possibilities for searching out new relationships between her life and the environments that she inhabits.

Migration is a rite that confers a status worldwide. It joins all of those who have experienced it, regardless of their past or present social position, their level of educational attainment, or their wealth. Sometimes it is forced; often it is planned for many years; sometimes it is attempted and then abandoned. But in any case, the experience of a first migration can become like a territory of the imagination. When someone migrates a second time, or a third, what they leave behind is less their birthplace than immigration itself.

CHAPTER 4

PULLING ONESELF TOGETHER

Generally speaking, the central episodes are detached, as though they are floating in a space that at times obeys the rules of perspective and at others is articulated according to the laws of the association of surfaces. One must not think that the profound connection of these distinct compositions resides in a certain way of looking at the world and of transferring it along with its particular laws onto a two-dimensional surface. On the contrary, what links the episodes to one another are the intellectual elements of the relationship between places and times that everything in the world separates. This separation does not result in the works having an unrealistic, artificial, or arbitrary character.

The links of causality combine the episodes and the details of the work in the memory to evoke a satisfactory global image. . . . If the "Hours of Boucicault" can be considered one of the first great works of modern painting . . . it is not because the author made reference to this or that detail in an illusionist manner—the changing sky, the twilight, etc.; it is due to this setting up of differentiated relationships of fragments that are ordinarily isolated, foreign to one another in visual experience.[1]

—*Pierre Francastel on the Book of Hours of Boucicault*

IF A "SATISFACTORY GLOBAL IMAGE" can take form in the minds of those viewers of an illuminated manuscript who know the story of Christ's birth, sacrifice, and resurrection, the subject who makes herself by tying together countries has no such referential text or collective memory to depend on. Like the pictures assembled in the Book of Hours, the places that become life chapters sequentially mingle principles of composition, each country an image and an experience that is distinct, even though it mixes modes of representation that have become increasingly universal. The illuminated manuscript relies on knowledge of a story that is familiar to most viewers; even in the absence of a shared culture or language, even in the absence of belief, the general progression of the story of Jesus has been widely disseminated.[2] The global image thus includes an exemplary narrative of a life, a way of connecting the disparate pictures in the book. Serial migrants have no such story or collective memory.

While migration is a recognized rite of passage, the ideal immigrant is one who disappears by being integrated into the social fabric over time. The elements brought together by serial migrants—the "places and times that everything in the world separates"—are defined by borders. Yet these same lines of demarcation divide serial migrants among and within themselves. One might be considered an exile or a refugee, an immigrant or an illegal alien, at different moments in life or by different agents or others. The criteria for these designations are inconsistent. The process of achieving a "satisfying global image" from the collection of life intervals is arduous because the common story is obscured. The piecing together of a life story becomes the work of the subject, who relies on the lines of demarcation that isolate him (borders) as a means of finding a consistent point of reference.[3] Serial migrants are always subjects of states. They recognize that being allowed to settle anywhere is a privilege; someone can avoid or try to leave countries whose political or economic practices impede his ability to figure himself in ways he can live with, or he might seek out a place where he can more readily take action that corresponds to his own ambitions or sense of moral responsibility. But ultimately the associations one makes among life territories, and the designation one lives with as a refugee or an immigrant, an exile or an undocumented alien, are controlled and compelled by international law, bilateral and regional agreements, and states' migration policies, which often conflict.

Seyla Benhabib writes that today "we are like travelers . . . navigating an unknown terrain with the help of old maps, drawn at a different time and in response to different needs."[4] Even in this changing world, however, borders persist: migrants are nothing without "old maps." Although some frontiers have dispensed with guards, others are marked by high walls or electrified barbed-wire fences and patrolled by vigilantes. In any case, at every instance, to cross into a new country is to enter a series of systematically different relationships among the elements that make up the world as a whole. Serial migrants take borders seriously; borders are their defining element. These subjects are defined by taking on the diversity of efforts to systematize social life and cultural forms in bordered territories as a part of their own progression. Whether they embrace their subjection to the different definitions of who they are in various homelands or fight to dispel them as false, their struggle with the accumulation of truths about themselves according to successive social and political systems is part of the particular "truth-generating process" that characterizes this form of life.

Serial migrants make their life intervals of the modern political imagination with its framed ideals of the perfect association of territories to peoples and cultures. State lines, which accentuate the systematic aspects of place, define the stages of their lives. Yet adding up homelands leads them to a series of confrontations with the logic of accrual that overwhelms politics in our capitalist system. One might imagine it desirable to seek to add up the lessons learned about diverse cultures and political systems as a means of increasing one's cultural capital. However, in a time when the dependence of the polis on the *oikos* is taken for granted, when a market logic encourages forms of circulation that can seem overwhelming for the government of the self or society, serial migrants seek ways to limit this accumulation. They hang on to borders as a means of self-clarification. The literalism of this employment enables them to take progressive liberties of expression in action. Working with such commonplaces at their most essential to develop one's own story enables a subject to engage the different forms of politics that traverse the places of his life. An initial setting out of one's experience in terms of state territories and systems does not imply that a subject fails to understand that state sovereignty is relative or that social life cannot be bound to maps. It does suggest an effort to make order amid the accumulation of truths about oneself that are proffered most often in terms of this or that national system or cultural context.

Those who take the time to listen to serial migrants' stories are often captivated by their descriptions of diverse landscapes, impressed by their knowledge of multiple languages and the customs of exotic peoples, amazed by the slide show of a life that displays such intimacy with so many locations. Yet the accretion that can make someone's life fascinating is also a perpetual threat to the subject and a potential distraction for the analysis of her multinational life. For although it is tempting to imagine the serial migrant as a collector of countries, a patchwork subject, or an artist of *assemblage*—to portray him as a master *bricoleur*—would be to ignore the fact that simple collection cannot confer value or enable one to determine a course of action.[5]

From the immigrant's concern with the self as other, the serial migrant turns to the challenge of reconciling multiple ways of being another not only to others but to oneself. No one makes a life of exploring the variations in the rules of social and political games in general, but serial migrants associate them in themselves and link them in their lives. Even in the midst of living under or through a system, one progressively evaluates this process. Past experience and the knowledge of further intervals of life on the horizon interfere in this quest to define the self; the serial migrant uses borders to open gaps among several versions of the self, engaging a progressive dynamic of evaluation. Judgments among selves and the systems that generate them are necessary to self-clarification and action, yet this clarification is perpetually endangered by further accumulation. This may explain why serial migrants tend to overemphasize the systematic aspects of state action and the idea of a culture as an integrated composition. We (I include myself among them) draw on these divisions of place to develop a life story, an indication of the ways we have come to move with and through several truths to be true to ourselves, to be authentic, or at least continuous.[6] This process is not an abstract comparison of systems. It points to certain changes in the politics of our time that recall Foucault's analysis of the transformations of the late Roman Empire. He writes:

> Whereas formerly ethics implied a close connection between power over oneself and power over others, and therefore had to refer to an aesthetics of life that accorded with one's status, the rules of the political game made it more difficult to define the relations between what one was, what one cold do, and what one was expected to accomplish. The formation of oneself as the subject of one's own actions became more problematic.[7]

While some people reacted to the loosening of the clear path toward self and social realization through more flamboyant displays of the marks of their status and power over others, a holding on to symbols of disappearing prerogatives and positions, others let go of inherited measures of worth. These people sought further independence from the social order and sovereignty over themselves through what Foucault calls a "pure relation to the self."[8] One might imagine some migrants as moving in search of this kind of purity while others seek out a new location where they might more readily associate their personal convictions with the system in place. In either case, migrants of all kinds lead us to notice that there is a global hierarchy evolving in which the ability to move unimpeded is a sign of status. Serial migrants use borders to stage performances that point to this simple fact.

STICKING TO BORDERS

Alex was born in Romania and has lived in Lyon, Los Angeles, Teheran, Paris, Manama, Bucharest, and Istanbul. Years ago he could easily have applied for French or American citizenship, but he has held on to his Romanian passport even though, as he puts it, "I sometimes feel stopped in accomplishing many things because of the passport I am holding." Alex's French is impeccable; he speaks English with a perfect American accent. He has also mastered Persian and studied Arabic. With his up-to-date wardrobe and easy style of interaction, he moves effortlessly in the most exclusive circles of the art world in the United States, Europe, and the Middle East. Explaining his reasons for maintaining his Romanian passport, he notes "the changes within Europe during my back-and-forth voyages that started in the early 1990s, especially those regarding nationality":

> I was always carrying a Romanian passport, and while in the beginning of my travel I was permanently regarded with suspicion by the authorities, now it turns out that people in Western European countries do not even know if Romania is in the EU or not . . . I made a point not to apply for or change my citizenship, a personal political stance in order to bring to the surface the absurdity of the "national order of things."

At first, Alex developed his own performance as the citizen of a former Eastern Bloc country. Could a Romanian be so well dressed? His passport conjured up images of a divided Europe. Then there was a period of uncertainty; had Romanians become European? Now, with the flood of migrants since the opening up of borders, Alex's performance as a Romanian is projected against what border guards and ordinary European citizens observe in their countries. They see Romania as groups of penniless musicians in the Paris metro, immigrant laborers in Germany, or pimps who commandeer bands of children to pick pockets in Rome.[9] These images frustrate many Romanians, including "ordinary" Romanian immigrants, because in them Romania's internal divisions and embarrassments are exhibited. There is widespread disdain, for instance, of the many Gypsies who have fled their country because of merciless persecution and poverty.[10] Alex takes all of this onto himself to fashion a self-presentation that provokes questions about the diverse truths about his country. His hanging on to his passport and pushing his nationality makes a spectacle of how borders militate against diversity.

Alex sees his insistence on a single passport as a comment on the persistent inanity of the nation-state system. Yet this expressive choice has had far-ranging consequences for what he can become or accomplish. His mobility in spite of his passport shows that he has the ability to cleverly "work" not one but several systems, not only to settle in the places of his choice but to become accomplished at their cultural repertoires and gain status according to their criteria. He has earned several advanced degrees, published articles and books in two languages, hosted a television program on fashion, been a lecturer at two universities. Surely such a history of high-status positions must have border-crossing value for the bearer? Yet certain doors remain closed to him. His opportunities for action are limited by an ongoing willingness to experiment with the self as accumulation in terms of the limits put on his action by progressive encounters with borders. This construal of the self and the value of life contradicts the very idea of strategic self-cultivation associated with social mobility.

Alex's accumulation of experiences seems a rebuttal to the way in which the international economic system increasingly makes the self a site for accruing capital, whether economic or social. He is of many places, but what does he have to show for it? Might his mode of action, his mastery of the art of accumulation to shape a self defined by values that contradict the kinds of choices migrants are assumed to make on the road to the "good life," be a rejection of the tendency to turn one's qualities into profit? Might Alex's life be an ongoing critique of capitalism after all?

Marc, who was raised in France and lived for many years in Israel before becoming a student and then a teacher in Morocco, is an example of fullness: of figure, of appetites, and of a kind of odd ambition that doesn't quite translate in conventional terms and might make some people say he is full of himself. Like many North African Jews, his parents fled the region of their ancestors at the close of the colonial era. Now his presence in a North African country where only a small Jewish community remains recalls the importance of the Jewish role in the Maghreb's history.[11] He lives as a reminder, a remainder. As a man out of place, he seems to be trying to twist the arm of history. "He invests his presence with meaning by representing the Jew and Israeli in Morocco," Shana Cohen writes in her essay on Jewish serial migrants. "Marc strives to present an argument for some Israeli actions while demonstrating that Jews/Israelis possess a range of political opinions."[12] His return to Morocco, ironically, evokes the right of all Jews to return to Israel. His remarks also lead me to recall Leila's understanding of the continuity of the Mediterranean; the landscape that she says disappeared when her beloved Tangiers was "moved to the East." One might tease out the continuities of the self by stretching a lifeline across places that offer distinctive possibilities for figuring oneself as a certain kind of person. One might provoke history through a process of coming to terms with accumulation, not just of the cultural practices, political systems, or media of any one location now, but with the different ways that identities evolve historically. Some of the ways one has been a particular kind of person in the past may only be located in the memories of those who cohabited at a certain time in a given place. The collection of places that compose the self includes not only recollections but commentary about the direction history has taken.

One might recall that Leila interprets her serial migration as being motivated by the shifting of Tangiers to the "East," an abstraction of the sights and sounds and shared landscapes that shaped her childhood and made her hometown part of the Arab world. At home, Leila's talk animates a Tangiers that is as much a projection of an ideal conception of society as it is a return to the place of her childhood, but in public— even so far from Morocco, even now that she is a Canadian citizen— other immigrants assume things about her that she has made a life of rejecting. A page from my notes may serve as an illustration:

> It's starting to snow as I enter an athletic center in Laval with Leila and her ten-year-old son, Salim. As we are enveloped in the warm steamy air of the overheated gym, a woman calls to us loudly, enthusiastically; she salutes us in Arabic with warmth that makes me think she must be a close friend. But I notice that Leila's reaction to her is cold. As the woman moves toward us, accompanied by a boy, she speaks rapidly, excitedly, in Lebanese Arabic. Leila whispers to me that this is "George's mother," then responds to the woman's effusions with a polite "*Bonjour*." George's mother responds to Leila's French with a flood of questions about Leila's health and family, she in her dialect. Leila switches to English. "Hello, how are things with you and your family?" she inquires. Her interlocutor becomes flustered at Leila's apparent unwillingness to engage in conversation in Arabic. I begin to feel uncomfortable. Why is Leila making things so difficult? I ask myself. In spite of my very limited knowledge of Lebanese, I try to intervene: I offer greetings in standard Arabic to the Lebanese woman. But my efforts are rebuffed; she simply looks again at Leila and continues talking to her. She adjusts her speech to a more "standard" form of the language, to which Leila nods before ending the linguistic standoff by pointing me toward the locker room. Only once Salim was dressed and safely in the hands of his swimming instructor did she express her irritation: "This kind of thing happens all of the time here. People from the Middle East assume that I can understand them. Because I am named Leila they can't imagine I don't speak their kind of Arabic. They think I'm putting on some kind of pretense; if they only speak more loudly or with more classical words, I might reveal myself for the kind of Arab they imagine me to be. I know that that woman can't speak fluent French, but she doesn't even try. She speaks English with the swimming teacher and everyone else, so why can't she speak English with me?"

Leila's lack of knowledge of Arabic is a symptom, not the cause, of her progressive self-making. She learns languages easily. Her refusal to learn or understand forms of Arabic other than the dialect of North Africa is a protest; by refusing to communicate in Levantine Arabic or learn the "standard" variety, she remains the person who left home because shifts in the map deprived her of her birthright as she conceives it. Her ease of expression in so many tongues only serves to highlight her loyalty to a certain conception of the truth of her homeland. At the sports center Leila imposes the literalness of borders on George's mother, limiting communication to French and English, Canada's official languages.

Canada offers Leila some systematic advantages that many other homelands would not. She uses the country where she has become a citizen to dispute a version of the truth about herself that would limit her possibilities for self-definition. By rejecting Arabic as a connection, she does not leave Morocco behind but resists tying it to the Middle East. She evokes the double truth of herself in France, where being recognized as an immigrant tended to go hand in hand with being seen as an Arab or Muslim. With her perfect diction in the French of France, her Arab surname, her excellent English, and her hard-to-place Mediterranean looks, she is able to express herself through Canada in ways that are closer to the truth of herself as it might be observed in her multilingual living room. At home she can maintain her projective nostalgia for Tangiers; anyone who comes to the door might get a whiff of peppers roasting on the stove, and if invited inside, he might notice that the dark, heavy wood furnishings are reminiscent of living rooms he may have visited in Southern Spain or France, although a number of the posters on the wall bear titles in English. If he were invited to dinner, it would begin with a long, slow cocktail on the back patio, with homemade tapas. During Ramadan these might be replaced with the Moroccan soup known as *harira*, which, should he care to, he might drink before sundown, after which those who have chosen to fast sip it as their "breakfast." One might notice all of the "clues" that indicate the cultural references of Leila's life and add them up to make Leila out as an exemplar of the tolerant, multicultural subject one might expect a place like Canada to attract. What remains invisible in Leila's case is that a personal style and lifestyle have been progressively fashioned by a force of decision, indeed, by efforts at political theorization that have led her to exclude certain possible elements from her life and sense of self.

Alex uses his passport as a means to prod history and question its direction. Leila moves against the construal of herself as an agent in the process of regionalization that displaced her hometown and made her a migrant. The emphasis on the abstraction of borders leads to underscoring the importance of experience in making one a continuous subject. The syncretic tendencies that might seem to shape Leila's living room or Alex's performance are highlighted for the very selective strategies they are. Each works with a restricted palette to refine their line of action; only after a careful selection of colors do they develop the mixtures and tones that constitute their style.

Giorgio Agamben draws on Walter Benjamin's sense of history to assert that "history is not, as the dominant ideology would have it, man's servitude to continuous linear time, but man's liberation from it; the time of history and the *cairos* in which man, by his own initiative, grasps favorable opportunity and chooses his own freedom of the moment."[13] These performances indicate how borders might persist even beyond the liminal moments of migration's flight, bringing a certain freedom into the present. What Heidegger calls the *Augenblick*, a flash or breakdown, might be provoked by border crossings, but it can also be triggered by all kinds of social situations, inciting the subject to awareness of itself. David Couzens Hoy notes that in "the authentic present attitude of Augenblick, I project a meaningful course of action and I resolve, without relying on any external or extraneous input, to live my life in a coherent and connected way," in contrast to "the inauthentic present attitude," which is "to sit back and wait for time to pass for things to happen."[14] The serial migrant seeks out "extraneous input" not in the manner of a butterfly hunter who would capture multiple versions of the self to make a collection, but as part of a process of understanding his connections to others so as to enable self-definition. Using passports and assumptions of ethnic belonging and other such conventional means, one might turn commonplaces in unusual directions and thus demonstrate freedom.

Still, to notice that accumulation is meaningful only because it can lead to self-expression through the rhetoric of displacement is not sufficient; one needs to consider the extent to which the accumulation of "extraneous input" might lead to a history that is never fully apparent in a particular gesture, performance, or interaction. History is not merely what happened, then what happened next, with serial migrants framing life periods by shift of territory. To gain a better understanding of Alex's and Leila's performances, one needs to examine how the tying together of places in a life is a process of making experience that is never solitary yet exceeds the way that individuals are generally associated to the collective in social analysis. It is time to consider the process of transformation of a series of life intervals into a story, an experience and a world that might be expressed in the kinds of efforts Alex makes to hold on to his passport or how Leila draws on the linguistic borders of Canada to demonstrate her lack of complicity with the way Europe and the Arab World conspired to deny the truth of her birthplace.

FROM A SERIES TO A WORLD

Martine writes:

> In North Africa, I was too Catholic.
> In Peru and Colombia—I was physically too different (I am 5' 9" and blonde). My education and my economic background helped me to be successful in those countries but not to get integrated.
> In England I was always too French.

In the US, I feel comfortable and I am socially integrated but I do not feel at home with Americans who have not traveled internationally.

In France I feel at home but I do not feel comfortable (French are too narrow-minded, the economy is too slow). I do not feel socially integrated either (I only have foreigners as friends and my coworkers used to say I was too Americanized).

What makes a home?

Home is where I live.

My comfort and peace of mind.

Martine holds conventional political frameworks steady to explain something about herself. She notes that life in certain places caused her to pay special attention to her religion, physical appearance, education, economic status, or nationality. The specific lack of fit or ease of action she experiences in each location leads her to highlight some of the systematic differences among her homelands. One dramatizes these differences in order to sort oneself out. Self-reflection of this kind entails an assessment of the ways in which one's homelands offer systematic forms of identification, exclusion, possibilities for action or for relationships.

Collecting oneself in terms of systems joined by a life of progressive settlement encourages the subject to pay attention to himself both as a practicing representative of several homelands and as a free agent. But how does this effort to fit in progress? How does not quite fitting in, over time, lead to a peace of mind made of discomfort? How can a series of uncomfortable situations become a history that engages the truth of the self as a continuous, authentic subject, to make a place of "where I live" thanks to a "comfort" that comes from "peace of mind"?

Fiona, who made peace with Japan after her becoming brave scared away Japanese cockroaches, eventually left the country for Hawaii with her American husband, Brandon. Then they settled in London with their two children. Now in their thirties, Fiona and Brandon are preparing to move back to New Zealand. From a narrative about her first migration that focused on adaptation to a new environment, she shifts to a comparison of different "systems":

> Yeah, I see coming to the UK as a nice primer for me to move back to New Zealand because of the free education and health care. Brandon is so upset that he cannot go home for a visit without health care insurance. I really want to see that new Michael Moore film, "Sicko," because it is so bad for your (US) citizens medically when you have the money to do it (provide health care) and you don't. Where do we want to raise our family? In the USA we pay less taxes but get no services, in the UK or in New Zealand we pay more taxes but if we get hit by a car we don't have to worry about going bankrupt. My friend was in an accident and he received $100,000 to start a business when he got better from the state in New Zealand so that he could still be productive. You don't want to worry about these things when you walk down the street. I am so worried about health care in America. Even if you have it and get sick and lose payments, what is the point? This is putting us off to mainland America as is the whole competitiveness in schools. At university in America it is such a class system. You have to go to a special school to have a good life. . . . young people feel that pressure and they want to go to the "best" or else they are not considered smart. In New Zealand, if you want to be a doctor you go to university. You do not need to go to private preschool to go to Harvard.

Her thoughts move forward with increased alacrity. She does not plan to stay indefinitely in New Zealand; indeed, she already has plans to return to Europe, envisioning her children's future memory:

> I keep thinking it would be great to live in Europe again. The baby won't remember it. We're going to have to come back. If I go back to New Zealand I could probably get my Masters in Social Work because I'm sure I could get another work visa to the UK but we could do it when the kids are in school. As they get older we could do more in Europe. To be able to find a job in Europe at this level of our careers is very difficult because we don't have careers. We tell ourselves we will be in New Zealand for 5, 6, 10 years. We do want to give it at least five years. We gave Hawaii four, we can give New Zealand five.

Fiona's musings bring to mind Michael Oakeshott's comments on the problem of making a chronology into a history. "If, then, we conceive history as a 'series,' we are nevertheless obliged to admit that in this so-called historical series the terms are not merely successive, they offer criticism of one another," he remarks.

> They do not stand isolated and self-evident, but are guaranteed by the series as a whole. What comes later in the series is part of the ground upon which the historian establishes what comes earlier, and *vice versa*. In short, it is impossible to exclude criticism from history, and where there is criticism there is judgment. Before a 'recorded' event becomes an 'historical' event, a judgment must have been interposed. But judgment involves more than a series, it involves a world. And the view that history is concerned with what is merely successive breaks down.[15]

Fiona's proposed places of future life are tied to the limitations of language, to reflections on what she or other family members might become under different ways of organizing collective life and conceptions of status. Her ideas about these "systems" are thus not simply abstract; they take into account that submitting oneself to a form of government or set of debates about what makes a good society is conditional. The "systems" that state lines frame are not judged solely in terms of how they might provide a social position for an individual or a family. They are assessed in terms of their relationship to imagined projects and particular stages of life. The elements for a good life change, as do health care, education, and economic opportunities in particular countries. What is "best" at a given point in time might depend on whether one is single, whether one has children, and whether one seeks further education, as well as on the evolution of a polity or a region. The evolving family life is marked by judgments of value as they relate to location, but not through a singular valorization of a static, homogeneous, or hegemonic system that sets the terms for the accrual of economic, cultural, or social capital.[16] Fiona's discussion of past and potential places of her life shows how the subject of migration can become collective. The ongoing story of the family must be conjugated with the lives of the individuals. Including everyone in the experience of history becomes a preoccupation.

REPEATED RETURNS

Even when "choice" is too strong a word to describe the reasons for making a life of repeated migrations, the subject who settles progressively makes sense of herself dynamically. While the periods of her life are marked by her serial migrations, the series needs to be made into a history in order to become meaningful. How might she develop a clear understanding of this process even though the lexicon of immigration and its trials deflects attention from her dilemma, sometimes seeing a solution in the very accumulation that plagues her? The immigrant may become of the places she inhabits, but surely not by simple addition. In a single lifespan serial migrants show the difficulty of sustaining a logic of hyphenated identity. Their "collection" of countries and readiness to adapt often make them incredibly knowledgeable; many speak several languages and have an insider's understanding of the places they have called home. But what of the inevitable confrontations among the values that make up any history and mark the systematic differences among the territories in the serial migrant's past? One might assume that a broader horizon for selecting one's homelands might lead to greater freedom in setting one's path, but this greater choice of destinations can actually heighten the problem of developing a clear sense of direction. Often, retracing one's steps becomes an important element in escaping the sometimes confusing process of accumulating accounts of oneself and enables one to develop a clearer sense of one's own truth.

To return to our own point of departure in this chapter, we recall that it is a shared narrative that unites the disparate scenes and distinct modes of rendering that shape the Book of Hours. The serial migrant needs to join scenes of a life by supplying "the intellectual elements of the relationship between places and times that everything in the world separates," as Francastel said of viewing the illuminated scenes.[17]

Some serial migrants develop a way of testing who they have become by returning to their place of birth regularly. One might think of this practice as a form of controlled comparison of the migrating subject. Hani pondered her partner Thierry's pattern of displacement:

> I'm thinking along that line lately not for myself but my partner. I observe some repetitive practice with him which relates to your idea of the liminal and interstitial space. He first moved from Paris to Hong Kong for a fresh breath away from his family. Then back to Paris (from Hong Kong) after 4–5 yrs due to homesickness. A short stay in Paris awoke his dislikes with the city and the family. Then he departed Paris this time to London. After 6 years or so, his homesickness is recalling him. He now wants to return to Paris, though this time with a clear sense of staying for a short while (and the next stop remains unclear). It seems that he prefers living elsewhere but needs to return "home" once for a while (to recharge? to regain a sense of identity? to reinforce "his home"?—I don't know).

If going home allows someone to "recharge" or "regain" himself, it is perhaps because returning to the point of departure allows for a clear and elegant closure of each chapter of a life. The birthplace is a kind of full stop; one uses it to punctuate the unfolding life. It is not simply a point from which to be born again; return holds out a promise of comparability. Holding the point of return steady, keeping one of the terms of migration constant, leads to using the repetition of life in an experimental spirit under conditions that, while not up to the standards of laboratory protocols, include more guarantees of replicability and reliability than many forms of scholarly social research. The procedure is dependable both in terms of the constancy of the instrument (the self) and the degree of knowledge of the analyst who has spent so many years coming to know the places thus joined. Naturally, the self of today is an instrument altered by the path taken yesterday. One has been changed by the passage and its experience, just as the history as a whole has been transformed. We might recall Hélène's awareness of how the "Paris of today" is not the one she lived in. Her reflections offer a word of warning about the way in which such a return might actually be problematic if it is sameness or "identity" one seeks. But regular returning to the point of departure can help to register these alterations when the birthplace maintains certain systematic continuities, as France has over Thierry's still young life.

But what about those who return home regularly not by choice, but because they are unable to find a place that will allow them to settle permanently? Although Maria completed a bachelor's degree in English literature in the Philippines, she has always worked as a domestic servant. In her twenties she moved to Germany to work for a diplomat's family.[18] When they were posted to the United States, she was unable to obtain work papers. She returned to the Philippines for a few months with the intention of securing a contract somewhere else. She found a job in the UAE, but after a few years in Dubai her contract ended. Once more she had to return to the Philippines before moving on. That is when she found her present position in Qatar; she has been able to remain in this position for over six years, although she had to return briefly to Manila after three years because her contract expired. It is difficult to maintain her residency status, but with the support of her employer she has managed it. Now, she contemplates where she may end up next; although she can always refuse a contract proposal, her choices are limited.

Maria enjoys short stays in the village where she was born but has no desire to ever resettle there; she could not "fit" there after so many years abroad. She prefers urban life but detests Manila because she finds it too "disorganized"; life there is "simply too difficult, even if one is well off." The capital city offers her a point of comparison with the other cities she has made her own, but also leads her to assess how her migratory projects have change her own situation. Now she could afford to live in Manila, if not luxuriously. She enabled her niece to attend university; she says she made herself that "kind" of person. In this sense, her return allows her to take the measure of the changes in herself, even though she resents having to make her birthplace and country of citizenship a touchstone for her life.

The star-shaped form that her trajectory traces on the map offers an image that suggests the centrality of the original homeland. But this configuration is not of her own choosing; it indicates that her decisions and judgments about how to associate the places of her life are made within the confines of a certain universal estimation of how a particular kind of person ought to be allowed to circulate. One might interpret this as a redoubling of the effort to maintain her in the situation of an immigrant, to blot out her history. Returning regularly to the point of departure, by choice or compulsion, might tend to have this effect even as it clarifies the comparisons among one's homelands, precisely because the punctuation of the birthplace reiterates its centrality in one's identity. Returning to the place one began seems to enable a certain sense of the linear progression of one's life, but in so doing it may impede one's ability to fully realize one's history as a drawing together of places, as one's experience of immigration. It is noteworthy that this arrangement mimes the shape of diplomatic life, with its recurrent resettlement in the home territory that serves as a reminder of what one represents. Perhaps especially when this form is chosen rather than imposed, it presents strange resonances with Nick Mai's errant youths, whom we met in Chapter 2. Their restless wandering only binds their imagination ever more securely to expectations of life in the patriarchal systems they seek to escape. But as Fiona suggests, one might return with the plan of staying for several years and then leaving again. One might also resettle in lands where one has been an immigrant.

Assad was an acquaintance of mine when I lived in Morocco in the

1990s. In Casablanca he worked at the same company as Leila, and eventually he, like Leila, would move with his spouse and children to Canada.[19] Assad was born in Egypt. Although his family was of modest means, he was a good student and completed an engineering degree. As a young man he received an offer for a job in Tangiers and decided to take it. Neither he nor the Egyptian woman who would become his wife had family in Tangiers or Casablanca, but they quickly made friends. They had a comfortable life and interesting work. They had their children there, and were very happy for a long time. But as the children grew older, they began to consider the disadvantages of not being able to become citizens and of finding it difficult to raise their children as Coptic Christians. In Morocco, citizenship is conferred by descent and naturalization is extremely difficult to obtain, requiring a *dahir* from the king. Although immigrants are free to practice their religion in Morocco, unlike Egypt and other Middle Eastern countries, there is no indigenous Christian community; the word that designates Christians, *nsara* (Nazarenes, followers of Jesus of Nazareth), is used as shorthand for "European." It is taken for granted that Arabs are Muslim.[20] As Assad's children grew older, their friends at school naturally expected them to follow Moroccan Muslim rituals. While being a categorical conundrum was not a problem for Assad or his wife, the children found it hard to live with the contradiction they seemed to pose for those around them. This led them to decide to move to Canada, where they could become citizens and where Christianity was the dominant religion. But Assad confided in Leila that if it weren't for the responsibility of raising his children, he would "leave for Morocco tomorrow." As he told Leila, "I spent the best years of my life in Morocco." He does not miss Egypt and would never contemplate returning there, although he does go back to visit his family. Sometimes he thinks about resettling in the United States. Who knows, he jokes—maybe when he retires he will move to "California," the most luxurious neighborhood in Casablanca.[21]

Rheinhilde did just what Assad dreams of doing. She was born in a part of Germany annexed by Poland after World War II. So although she grew up in Freiberg, she always had the feeling that she was an immigrant in her own country. She thinks this might be what led her to travel as a teenager, then to move to Kenya to conduct a research project while she was in college. It was in Nairobi that she met a Kenyan military officer whose family was from Goa. It was there too that they married and had two children. She felt at home there; like a "real" immigrant, she had no intention of ever leaving. But then her husband took a job with the United Nations. He did not want her to live in Nairobi with the children, and he persuaded her to leave her adopted homeland.

As she related the story, her tone was bitter, still tinged with anger. "He took me to the edge of civilization, to Canada, and dumped me there," she told me. The move to Edmonton was a prelude to their divorce. Even after they split up, Rheinhilde stayed on to raise the children. They felt totally at home there, but she never did, nor did she care to. She worked and had a social life, but as soon as her younger child completed high school, she immediately made plans to return to Nairobi. She was glad to be back, but the situation was difficult. Things had changed in the intervening years. Not only had her family by marriage emigrated, but the political climate had become unstable. She found it impossible to settle there permanently, so she devised a creative alternative: she expanded her second country to embrace a region.

Moving first to Sudan and then to a series of Persian Gulf states, she has found teaching positions that allow her to circle around her second country and make frequent visits there. In Bahrain or the UAE she often runs into people who, like herself, speak Swahili. In her spare time she studies Arabic, but her real passion has become the study of the historical connections between Africa's east coast and the countries of the Arabian Peninsula. The places of her life are thus not simply connected by a tie to a homeland; the choice to move to each new place is a result of strong ties to the place she chose first, as a young adult. Her further moves were generated by this scene of first immigration—the chapter of her life when she married and gave birth to her children. Although her stay in Canada was lengthy and although her children still reside there, her second homeland remains the compass for her life path as well as the guiding thread of which she weaves her lifeline.

We have seen the importance of the first migration as a rite of passage, as a defining part of what every serial migrant repeats with each move between one place and another. The first migration is also a time before the introduction of the horizon of further displacements. One might register its dramas, suffer from its in-betweeness, but one might also consider it a state of naiveté or ignorance, a time before the single-minded relationship of host to home was torn asunder, before the demands for loyalty to one's "parent" nations had to face the challenges of multiplicity; a time when nationality felt natural or chosen, in any case, serious. As though to mirror this situation of divided but "natural" ignorance, the first migration is often associated with one's younger self. It is the place one traveled to first, the place that made one an immigrant, sometimes in spite of oneself. People's voices often take on a wistful tone when speaking of their second home in spite of all the difficulties and discomforts they may have endured there. It was the move to that place, and nowhere else, where they experienced the initiation of the immigration journey that had led them to the present. The one complicating factor for Rheinhilde was that she felt like an immigrant in Freiberg, but no one perceived it. Perhaps the first move to Kenya was a homecoming already, a coming-out as an immigrant.

In Rheinhilde's case, it was also the place where she married and became a mother. In Kenya she felt at home not only with the place but in her marriage; when the relationship was "moved," it failed. Her serial migration was decided for her, and she still resents her husband for making the decision to settle in Canada. Her story illustrates the fact that while the forward motion of the basic narrative of serial migration progresses in abstraction, certain territories thicken in their meaning for the life as a whole. They take on a special explanatory power and one often seeks to return to them, sometimes only in the imagination. The progress through the intervals or territories of one's life is also a movement through the stages of life. One returns, but one is older; perhaps one dreams of inviting one's grandchildren to visit a homeland one came to know oneself as a young woman.

To return can be an uncanny reiteration of immigration; it calls into question what one has done in the many intervals that may have accrued since the time one first crossed that particular border. It forces an engagement with how history has altered even the location of the place one left perhaps decades previously. The trail of one's life augments the sense of difference produced by apparent return to sameness. Rheinhilde's making of a coherent world out of her own experience is very much in line with Oakeshott's understanding of how we make history from a series:

> What was taken for a mere series has turned, in our hands, into a world. For, whatever the terms of a "series" so far lose their isolation and come to depend upon the criticism and guarantee of other, perhaps subsequent, terms, and of the "series" as a whole, there is no longer a mere series of what is successive, but a world of what is co-existent.[22]

The world Rheinhilde offers up is not simply one of narrative advancing or the persistence of an attachment to the country that made her an immigrant even as it made her a mother. Her return is a map in progress, a kind of message of hope to anyone who lives in exile. She circles around a country whose citizens act as doormen or waiters in the places she lives in lieu of Kenya; might speaking Swahili with them insulate her from the unjust reduction of people to functions associated with their origins? It is worth noting that the motions by which she extends Kenya mimic the way the territories of the Gulf region circle around Saudi Arabia. As she expands her world, through her actions figuring herself in response to an international order by using "old maps" she makes her life using the forms of Realpolitik. She works with the enduring myths and commonplaces of international relations to develop a highly personal world order.

CHAPTER 5

PRESENT CONTINUITIES

INTERNATIONAL LIFE is composed of five canvases. Though large, it is easily disassembled, boxed up, carried in a suitcase: it was rearranged to fit the cover of this book. The collage includes several colors of newsprint, scribbles, and photographs. Events, conditions, and actions float in a wash of rust and aqua that cuts the image vertically. A sapphire band is fed by a stream that appears to flow down toward a sky-blue lake, or perhaps it is a genie emerging as smoke from a magic cerulean lamp, the wishes he might grant protecting the dream world from the bright orange environment where conversation erupts in the shape of a broken tower or a missile. In the bright public space, English-language ads for houses in southern France mix with Arabic headlines about nations at war; a masked man hangs upside down while making the news. The obituary of a once famous opera singer is splashed in turquoise, intimating how music can evoke that other dreamworld of sea and night and unseen beings, a signal of how public worlds partake of intimate flows of thought that jumble time in ways difficult to put into words.[1]

In contrast to a book of hours that brings together multiple representations of an iconic life intellectually, this mundane record of a private existence shows the flow of a single cloth interrupted. Five panels, consistent in tone, broken into regular intervals by the edges of the canvases, coax the eye into a saccadic rhythm to bring the whole into focus. The completeness of the image emerges from breaking up what is continuous; each panel is an interval of sight, a momentary resting point on the path of the eye that sweeps upward to rest on the touch of fingers on the back of a hand.

Sitting across the table from the anthropologist with her notebook or tape recorder may trigger memories of the moment when one crossed a border or touched a brush to a white canvas; one gathers one's thoughts to reflect on one's life, one seeks to express one's biography as a continuous gesture or to account for changes in plot in ways that seem logical. Images and letters, memories and reveries that make up one's experience are ordered in succession to tell one's story. In contrast, *International Life* evokes the tangle of words and images, facts and emotions, reminiscences and feelings that intermingle in the present in an internal conversation that is difficult to translate into narrative. The continuity of the subject is always more than can be said, one's history more than a set of choices and deliberations. Evidence of who one is now, made up of pasts seemingly forgotten or left to the side, sometimes erupts into present consciousness; one might observe one's own hand gesturing in a manner that brings some place of the past into the room uninvited, or register a word uttered with an accent that adds to the meaning for oneself but for no one else who is present.[2]

Drawing out modernity's most persistent myths about the relationship of collective life to territorial divisions as a form of life punctuation is not sufficient to explain what holds a life together. The homeland is a means of marking time, but it is also a structure that, like Bachelard's house, "generates its counsel of continuity."[3] Each country of settlement, with its mapped borders and system of government and claims to cultural uniqueness, strives to portray itself as a singular experience, a self-enclosed context. Moving among homes leads us to dwell on how this process of self-figuration of the nation, state, and culture occurs in terms of the possibilities each homeland opens up for self-development. Through the ensuing process of self-definition we notice continuities among places that are distant, facilitating our own coherence, even while the interruptions of borders allow us to make ourselves anew.

Picking up and moving when one is living a materially comfortable life, settling where one's previous work goes unrecognized, seems explicable only if one has a clear direction and purpose. For those who perceive the value of travel and resettlement as a means of gathering knowledge, experience "abroad" may be seen as widening someone's perspectives even without such a specific aim or calling. But serial migrants settle for so very long. They get mired down in places others dream of escaping. To explain displacements by reference to an evolving career makes sense. But even to people who are open-minded and tolerant of difference when it comes to others in their midst, someone who makes an experiment of his life for no good reason, leaving one comfortable situation after another behind without a clear goal, must appear strange. The difficulty of understanding moving with no obvious goal, moving for reasons that remain unspecified, can result in serial migrants' becoming objects of suspicion; people assume they harbor hidden motives. Their ongoing mission or objective must be disguised. One might interpret such a precarious lifestyle as inspired by some higher cause, some religious or ideological fervor.

Nur explained that she struggled with questions of identity as a young woman of Italian and Indian parents growing up in Italy. At thirty-five she embarked on a series of migrations that took her from Europe to Latin America, Asia, and the Middle East. Over time she learned that integration means that "you accept your destiny and feel contented with where you are without torturing yourself with endless nostalgias that in my opinion are not actually related to places, but to phases of life, of different 'you's' in different stages . . . 'you's' that you must learn to let go as you change and grow." But ultimately her quest led her to see the relativity of all earthly engagements. Twelve years ago, Islam "found" her and she made a "second migration," one that enabled her to let go of all of those nostalgias that plague us if we concentrate solely on our earthly life. Now, where she lives or what she accomplishes has become a matter of little importance; she sees that life on earth is only a prelude to eternity.[4] But it is only in retrospect that this perspective emerges to shape our reading of Nur's story. Now, looking back, we understand that the strangeness of the serial migrant, the haunting intensity of engagement in too many places, is sometimes perceived to be loosened by an act of grace. With Nur's "second migration" the awkward search for the self through serious engagements with many places and possible selves ceases. But for others, including those for whom religious beliefs are defining elements in their lives, the search for fulfillment gives meaning to their actions in each place they dwell.

Shana Cohen writes, "I interpret my work for community development in the United States, Morocco, India, and England as linking my place, the place I have created for myself in the changes my work initiates, with spiritual purpose."[5] For her, putting the principle of service to others into action is an expression of belief, and a sense of identity and belonging emerges in relation to this action, not from being part of a group in a particular locale. The places of life draw together in a continuous life location that evokes *makom*, the Hebrew word for place, which for the poet Jabès is a place of "revelation."[6] This revelatory space does not evolve through a verification of actions in terms of already known truths or rules. Rather, it comes about through the critical assessment of possibilities for conceiving or realizing a project of development for others and of the self in a present that includes an awareness of the nature of a quest, "the constant striving to arrive at the unreachable while dwelling in the cosmos," as Cohen puts it.

This sense of an unfolding truth resonates with the notion of fulfillment that Hayden White discerns as having inspired Eric Auerbach's magisterial study of reality in Western literature, *Mimesis*, which White conceives as typically modernist. He writes:

> The notion of fulfillment is crucial for understanding the peculiar nature
> of Auerbach's conception of historical redemption. It provides him
> with a modern equivalent of classical telos and a secular equivalent of
> Christian apocalypse. It allows him to endow history with the meaning
> of a progress toward a goal that is never ultimately realizable nor even
> fully specifiable. It gives him a concept of a peculiarly historical mode of
> causation, different from ancient teleological notions, on the one side,
> and modern scientific, mechanistic notions, on the other. This distinctly
> historical mode of causation I propose to call figural causation.[7]

On one hand are borders, separations; on the other is a sense of forward motion, dictated by an as-yet-unrevealed aim, as one moves across the borders seeking, coming to self-realization. Shana's belief unfolds through her efforts at self-development; there is no single moment of truth, no apocalypse, but instead a continuity of purpose through her work, even though it goes unrecognized by any organization or group, religious or secular. Indeed, the intensity and longevity of her involvement in many places can appear not only strange, but a provocation to received ideas about the kind of life path expected of someone with a private school education and prestigious diplomas. A continuity of purpose through work is one of the main ways that immigrants structure their lives and social relationships. Yet to take service seriously in the absence of support and recognition from some organization, some collective vision or deliberation, to interpret one's labor as something other than striving for the accumulation of capital or status, must seem very strange indeed.

The process of engaging in a scientific form of experimentation that takes into account how experience alters the self, its instrument, in a space of inquiry that unfolds by chance and choice might make sense for the anthropologist. Like the emblematic Kula shell, the anthropologist takes on value with the multiplication of sites and duration of fieldwork in a way that might be converted sooner or later into some kind of job position, academic or otherwise. But what of those who make of themselves an evolving field? Those who leave behind what is familiar to move to new homelands where they do not know what awaits them?

Many of the serial migrants I encountered who were working as cashiers, teachers, or taxi drivers had held jobs of much higher status in other locations; many changed careers or endured repeated reexaminations or retraining in their professions in each new home. These individuals whose experience has provided them with the very skills that might be rewarded in the increasingly international job market—flexibility and ability to adapt—often choose a lack of professional continuity. Or one might say that they employ their flexibility to their own ends. Instead of striving to move up the echelons of a company or a career, they often shift from one line of work to another. Some explain that they simply seek new experiences. But many others have their own plan that guides them: a project that is not as obvious to others. Developing the life story and ways of recounting it to oneself is perhaps especially important for people who make themselves of several homelands. The story includes one's family and one's friends, but even they may not grasp "the whole picture." The life Rheinhilde makes to turn a country into a regional commentary might be beautiful in its symmetry, but its contours are invisible except to the small circle of those who are privy to her history and motivations. Without public recognition, the ideas, beliefs, and convictions that move individuals might appear profoundly eccentric or even suspicious.[8] The congregation of fellow believers might hesitate to sanction one's motivations as emerging from convictions they share because it is not the result of collective decision, communion, or discussion. Such actions might seem so very particular, so out of context, so strange, that they are meaningless to others.

Margaret Archer notes that "contextual discontinuity" and "particularistic experiences" can make it difficult to articulate one's "internal conversation." She writes, "For those people who gradually learn that their internal conversations do indeed only 'make sense to themselves,' this discovery has far-reaching consequences."[9] Few sets of people seem to be more "discontinuous" in their dwelling places or more particularistic in their self-talk (insofar as we might guess its content) than serial migrants. One might see my project to follow them as inspired by an impulse similar to that which leads Archer to critique the way reflexivity is generalized in literature on modernity and post-modernity and her attention to the fact that reflexivity is important to all forms of society.[10] She too seeks to understand the way people might arrive at different ways of structuring their self-talk; but she understands mobility as a matter of positioning and moving ahead in an enclosed society the composition of which goes unquestioned. Given this background and context, the issue of location is unidimensional, even if the subjective response to it is not. This leads to a lack of awareness of the reflexive nature of the "contexts" themselves and a lack of attention to what makes society or politics, that is, particular forms of association and deliberation that associate subjects and offer them the possibility of making themselves with others. One must develop an understanding of how what brings people together also shapes the way internal conversations are shaped, and this means considering the strategic striation of states that are themselves partly nomadic; it involves a more fundamental questioning of the way that who we are is related to where we might go because certain locations enable specific kinds of meetings with others. A more general but not universal approach to mobility must be developed.[11]

Archer suggests that a person who suffers from being too "particular" due to unusual experiences is "thrown back on one's own mental resources."[12] But what are these resources? In accounting for the content of the flows of individual self-awareness, she follows Colapietro's account of Pierce in thinking that a subject's experience is widened and enriched by the accumulation of languages and public media she has been exposed to:

> When I enter into the inner world, I take with me the booty from my exploits in the outer world, such things as my native language, any other languages I might know, a boundless number of visual forms, numerical systems and so on. The more booty I take to that secret hiding place, the more spacious that hiding place becomes . . . the power and wealth of signs that I borrow from others and create for myself determine the dimensions of my inwardness.[13]

The accumulation of "booty" poached from multiple sources of public media might enable the individual to draw on "boundless visual forms and numerical systems," to realize some kind of individualized itinerary.[14] But this sense of the public world is passive; it assumes that one can just gather things without any intervening screens to filter meaning. It is devoid of the kinds of relationships with others that are part of "context" at its most meaningful. Since her research on reflexivity and social position is set according to the game board of British class society, alternative forms of self-reflection are set out in terms of the strategic moves of individuals as they advance as a pawn or a queen or change their attributes in a process that orients their self-reflection and ability to share their internal worlds with others. One might develop alternative values to those of the market, but these are responses to this closed context. Although Archer remarks that there are "new, young cosmopolitans" characterized by a "growing disembeddedness" that "coincides with a shifting opportunity structure," how such observations might challenge the very way one approaches the study of society remains outside the purview of the study of social mobility within state borders. The space of investigation cannot include them or explain how they recognize "opportunity." We are told that for these young professionals "socialization plays a negligible role in their course of action." But how can this be so?

It is not because conventional ways of theorizing about social life fail to account for something that it doesn't exist; even if one imagines these "new, young cosmopolitans" to be self-centered products of a global market always on the lookout for "opportunity," one cannot claim they have not been socialized. People who have lived through several homelands might be seen not as freed up by mobility, but as over-socialized. Settling sequentially might be conceived as contributing to social reflexivity. One's story is recounted as a narrative of moving through contexts; there is an abstraction of national territories, not the self. Experience evolves through moves that are both a shedding of contexts and a gathering of them so as to bring something of each into the future. One develops a story by noting borders, unfolds a life location by following and recognizing continuities of relationships that span one's homelands. This is not simply a matter of strategy or position or the collection of public media. Languages and public worlds and various accounting systems are certainly involved in making us who we are. But what are public media at a time when Abderahman's office is conceived in the image of the Arab League? When his immigrant media professionals imagine the Arab public in a Dubai studio financed by Saudi entrepreneurs, while they themselves experiment with a different experience of the Arab world in the social life among themselves? That public realm is unconnected from any place ruled by a state in which these journalists and managers and publicists might be "integrated" or become citizens. Yet, they participate in a highly strategic politics that might be symbolized by Al Arabiya's competition with Al Jazeera. While they are engaged in an effort to develop international standards of "proper" journalistic practices, there is something more politically essential in their efforts to shape the Arab region than can be rendered by reference to some Bourdieusian field of journalistic action. One must consider how accumulation questions context as well as how it is directed by political and economic movements.

It may be annoying to be mistaken for a "regular" immigrant or categorized according to a variety of ethnic, racial, or sexual criteria, but repeating these encounters in each of one's homes can actually be productive in the process of self-definition through public action, as Alex with his Romanian passport and Leila with her Moroccan Arabic have shown. Translation from one idiom to another is not really a problem; indeed, it can be a particularly helpful exercise in self-clarification. While successive settlement makes a convenient plot in one's life story, emphasizing that plot might make it more difficult to elucidate how one's experience is continuous, not simply because the self is a container for so many languages, images, or numerical systems but because each homeland is itself a strategic play on increasingly similar social worlds that span the globe. Different political systems favor the dominance of certain forms of social experience and notions of value that coexist everywhere. Indeed, one might consider how the differential composition of these shared elements could lead to new typologies of political systems or ideologies. Serial migrants have practical experience of how these different ways of coming together with others are encouraged or inhibited in different political landscapes. They notice how the present includes absences of the self they might welcome, tolerate, or reject. Yet they are less haunted by some framed, contained, total vision of the self in some former life, or perplexed by the task of pasting together the fragments of several such versions of who one is, than concerned with the ethical, aesthetic, or political valence of this selective invisibility. Following their efforts at self-continuity enables me to explore the global social worlds that together make up each country or city differently.

A CERTAIN KIND OF FOREIGNER

Even those who have chosen exile cannot simply disregard the way their birthplace colors their accent, the fact that a second or third homeland has altered their way of walking. There are continuities of self that are not of one's own choosing.

As Noha thinks about the future, she notes how different environments might bring out different aspects of herself. When she left Egypt in her twenties, she vowed never to return. Life in Cairo as a woman was intolerable. She married a Danish man and settled with him in Copenhagen, but being an Arab in Denmark became a problem. Moving to London "made that better," because it was a much larger, more diverse city with foreigners from all over the world. She thought that living in England with her second husband, who is English, and two daughters would give her a place in a warm family circle, but that didn't happen. She is now divorced and often feels stuck, but she dreams about the future, when her girls will be independent.

> I was on a work trip to Syria and Lebanon last February and for some
> reason I started thinking about relocating to one of those countries. . . .
> I was even surprised that I should think of moving back to the Middle
> East, but the advantage of an Arab country is that I'd still be able to "feel
> at home" and yet be a kind of exotic foreigner among the local people,
> because this is how I felt in Syria when I was there in February. I think
> the older I get, the more I need to be "at home," and since I cannot
> really go back home to Egypt, I feel the need to compromise this concept
> somehow, either by dreaming of an Arabic-speaking country but without
> the restrictions in the home of origin, or a country with promising
> network opportunities such as the USA (or so it is in my imagination,
> although I've never been to the States).

Although Noha chose self-exile, her birthplace resonates in her voice. The charming lilt of her accent evokes the films and songs of her native Cairo, recalling famous actors and politicians well known by anyone who speaks the language, due to that city's role as a center of media and politics. In Syria or Lebanon Noha can count on mutual comprehension and appreciation of her "exotic" turns of phrase. Yet for all of the allure of being both exotic and at home, of having some aspects of her chosen path publicly discernible in her accent, she sees this "compromise" Arab world in terms of an alternative. America looms as a land of "network opportunities," a chance to realize her potential as a professional. The choice is between, on one hand, a world in which she is marked by an audible difference that lends her an exotic charisma and, on the other hand, a world in which she might be measured by international standards to prove herself as a competent woman whose efforts and talents are recognized by those she has made her peers through her work.

Although Noha presents her future choice in terms of places that would emphasize different aspects of herself, the self is not measured in terms of position or a logic of capital accumulation, but in terms of two distinct modalities of public participation, two distinct modes of evaluation that already coexist in her present life. Her thoughts about the future enable her to recognize her present situation more fully; she realizes, for instance, that although it might be nice to relocate to another part of the country where life is less expensive than London—perhaps a rural area, since she adores the calm and beauty of nature—her present location is actually quite satisfactory: in London she can develop both her work and a social life that includes people who appreciate her jokes in Arabic.

Different places bring out the self differently through a process of revelation shaped by a reflection on how involvement in each might bring out the potential for relationships with other people, or the selves one might "import" from previous settlements. Although Majid holds Algerian nationality, he grew up in Morocco. After moving to France and staying there for a decade, he tried returning "home." He had a good, stable job and lived in a pleasant part of town. But as he and his wife began raising a family, he began to worry about the fact that his children were ineligible for the citizenship of their Moroccan mother.[15] And because of his experiences in France, he felt out of sync with the politics and values of his "home" country. Majid began to think about moving to a place where he, his wife, and their children could all become citizens. They decided to move to Quebec in the late 1990s. Life there has not been easy; although his wife has a steady job, Majid's employment over the last few years has been spotty in spite of his advanced degrees. Social interactions are not as "warm" as in more southern countries, and the winters are absolutely frigid. A friend in Rabat encouraged him to return "home." But, Majid says,

> in the course of the conversation I realized that my criteria for quality of life were not the same as theirs. For them, what's important is for example that when they wake up in the morning they don't have to prepare breakfast, they have someone to serve it to them. . . . I'm not judging them, but when I meet a beggar in the street first thing in the morning my entire day is ruined . . . but some others, they are immune to this. . . . One person's day might be ruined when he sees garbage all over the street, another will not even notice it, he will focus on other things, for instance, he will attach importance to the kind of car he drives, the kinds of furniture in his house. . . . As for me, I don't attach any importance to cars or furniture; I have lived in homes that are adequately furnished—that's it. . . . My childhood friends are in business, they own pharmacies, they teach at the university, and they are always telling me there is a quality of life in Morocco that one cannot find anywhere else, but one needs to complete the sentence—there are also unpleasant things one finds nowhere else. One has to make choices. One has to take on the risks involved in these inconvenient facts to have things like sun, an easy lifestyle, and enchanting weekends in Marrakech.

For Majid, quality of life does not stem from wealth; indeed, it requires a certain renunciation. The sacrifice Majid has made in terms of socially perceived status and position in the labor market surely goes unnoticed by most of those around him. His fervor for a particular kind of public life makes him equally a stranger to those in the country where he grew up and to those who assume migration is economically determined.[16] He has never been exiled for any political activity, nor is he politically active. Yet his attention to the way his own feeling of well-being arises—from a certain relation to shared spaces and a common understanding that everyone's basic needs must be met—points to how particular arrangements of politics work differently not only in relation to how they regulate the market, but also in how they encourage particular social interactions and experiences of the self. Majid derives a sense of direction not by strategic choices based on income but from noticing how different political systems might enable people to look each other in the eye.[17] His choice is not made in reaction to the eyes of the neighborhood but against the dominance of charismatic networks and values in monarchies.[18]

Maya explains that, where she lives now, it is her ongoing connection to herself—the self formed in other places—that allows her to remain sane. She and her husband grew up in Lebanon and left during the civil war for Martinique. Then they had the opportunity to take well-paid positions in the UAE. Yet, after seven years there, Maya is ready to move on. She is miserable. I invited her to dinner in a nice hotel, as I had done with other women the previous evening for interviews, but she had no appetite. She had a glass of wine and nibbled at a couple of olives while I excused myself for eating and said I was in the habit of eating dinner every night. My explanation felt like an admission of indiscretion or barbaric behavior. Like the other slender, attractive women I'd met in Dubai, Maya told me that she doesn't eat too much because she fears becoming overweight: "Like other women here, I fear losing my husband." She explained that in a place defined by the power of money, women police their appetites to try to maintain a measurably perfect figure. Those who are alone fear not being able to attract men, and those who are married fear losing them. Like many other women, she complains about the many "prostitutes, the young Russian girls with enlarged bosoms," who "don't hesitate to go after a married man."

According to her, everything here is a matter of counting. "I fear that over time my husband might be influenced by this lack of values in his private life," she said. She became tearful as she described her life, saying she doesn't eat because she could easily gain weight. She has a job, so unlike some women who do not work she says that she can't spend the day at the gym and the spa to keep in shape. Maya, like Miriam and Lisa and Rita and Sophia and Taghreed, all explained that in the UAE everything is determined by money. Workers are willing to put up with inhumane conditions for money, and money reduces women to a strange set of anxieties even if their figures do add up.

Maya says that in such an "empty" space, without a fixed population, one loses the sense of community that helps to give value to intimacy. In a place where money and getting ahead are all that bring people together, where everyone is an immigrant and even Arabic speakers like herself rarely know the "locals," one easily loses a sense of significant social connection. This makes her depressed; she wants to move again, back to Lebanon, or to Martinique, or perhaps to some new homeland. It is not a matter of lacking a sense of being "at home" with those who share a language, religion, or cultural tradition; indeed, everything is set up to reinforce such "community" feeling. The problem, she says, is that relationships among individuals both within and outside of the confines of the community are reduced to instrumental aims and economic gain. In Maya's view, it is perhaps not a bad thing to return often to one's homeland, as does Maria, who must return to the Philippines every few years. At least regular returns allow people to take the measure of the different places they have lived while retaining social ties to their birthplace. Maya especially regrets leaving her life in Martinique; she'd like to move there again or to metropolitan France, but she and her husband cannot obtain papers. In the final analysis, however, the problem is that her husband does not seem to feel the lack of social relationships that give value to life in the same way as she does. This is part of her frustration.

Maya's testimony about the emptinesses within herself, her attention to her looks, her lack of appetite, and her fear that the values of the marketplace might have invaded her marriage was similar to the testimony of many other women I encountered who had lived in various Gulf countries. They tended to recite a host of conventional complaints about the inauthenticity of life in the Gulf and its reduction of the common good to participation in work and consumption at the ubiquitous shopping malls, but what I found most interesting was the effect of this life, with the feelings of emptiness it produced, on women's relationships with their husbands, fiancés or one another. While economically motivated migration is often explained as being for the good of the family, and while the impact of migration on marriage can obviously be disastrous when one spouse leaves without the other, many women were made anxious by their suspicion that intimacy may be reduced by the relentless focus on money. It was not so much the economic logic of accumulation of capital they resented as the displacement of this means-to-an-end accounting into the private sphere.

CIRCLES, GRIDS, CONSTELLATIONS

As I listened to Maya's complaints and sensed her fear that bodily imperfection might cause the dissolution of her most intimate relationship, I could not help but think of the emergence of the "modern woman" as a fashionable figure in the twentieth century. I followed the history of this slender figure in my research for over a decade. In a region that stretched out from Casablanca toward Paris and Cairo, I explored her development in old women's magazines and in present-day beauty salons. This fieldwork in a location that developed in a mimetic relationship with my own evolving life of serial migration led me to notice that although this modern beauty seemed to be produced according to the same models and measurements everywhere, this similarity disguised important differences. Indeed, these differences could not be easily observed in terms of a style or price tag; differences became apparent through the way fashions were given value.

By exploring how apparently global recipes for beauty are given form in actual bodies in salons, I came to notice that it was how they are diversely judged that makes a difference. In different kinds of salons, individually or with others, one makes oneself by reference to distinct modes of evaluation that do not correspond to any pre-global national or cultural grounding. Three types of salons offer distinctive patterns of social interaction that "teach" those who enter them how to judge their own looks, the looks of others, and, more broadly, ideas and objects in the wider world.

How people get to salons is related to how they socialize there. Women usually walk to neighborhood salons—which I refer to as "proximate" salons—where they gather in circles to comment on one another's looks or share gossip about people they all know. In contrast, "celebrity" salons with famous hairdressers draw on a wide geographic area, and the relationships within them are focused on the client and her coiffeur, who approaches each woman as a work of art. The space of these salons expands to encompass other people at events where someone might appear as a unique creation of the famous coiffeur, and the coiffeur's name is joined to social constellations that gravitate around celebrities, either ones who are known worldwide or those of simply local fame. Salons in the third category, "fast" salons, promise speed and the competent reproduction of a particular look from a menu of styles. Interactions are mainly between a client and a beauty professional. Clients might travel some distance to get to a fast salon, but they generally like to get things done quickly and precisely; measurement is important, including the time it takes to complete the work (a client may be on a lunch hour or in a rush before picking up kids after school). All of these salons have a similar mission, essentially treating only one part of the body in the manner of modern medical specialization; they all employ measures similar to those Maya complains make it difficult to eat in Dubai, but they judge the results differently. One might graphically imagine these three associations of people as circles, grids, and constellations that move around in patterns determined by the gravity of the most powerful sun. Each site proposes a distinctive experience of social life, educating those who enter it in ways of evaluating not only beauty but conceptions of truth and justice.

Proximate worlds might be represented as a circle. The circle makes it difficult to hear any individual voice clearly; decisions are made and opinions developed by those gathered together. This is the world of close friends and relations that Maya misses in Dubai, although she tries to maintain it through the telephone and the Internet. This world does not promise equality to all its members, and it includes individuals who would not have been chosen as personal friends by others in the group. Age and education and reputation enter into the way in which people participate in this circle of collective evaluation and exchange. Proximate settings lead to judgments based on information gleaned from a variety of sources over many years, but it promises no lack of bias. This is a world of gossip as well.[19]

In contrast, the grid of a rational means-to-ends world develops the kind of measures one most readily associates with conversations among abstractly equal individuals, and the idea of "one man, one vote." A location of this kind brings people together to get a job done; they tend to evaluate one's work and worth according to universal standards and notions of fairness. This is a space where the potential for measuring social mobility and the generalizations of statistics take shape. Following Maya's account of her life, one might imagine Dubai as a place where this means-to-end rationality has gone wild, displacing every other manner of giving value to things or people. But this is also the world that enables Majid to express his desire to live with others in a place where each individual shares responsibility for the public space; where the street is kept as neatly as the house and no one ought to be in a position of subservience; where everyone might become a citizen.

Majid reacts to a world that dominates his birthplace, a world I characterize as a constellation. He expresses his idea of the good life by comparing his sense of public space and the value of objects with that of some of his friends in Morocco. They do not even see the beggar in the street. Their possessions are not simply measured in an accounting of their cost; for these friends, possessions shine with the kind of aura that Walter Benjamin attributed to objects of authentic art.[20] In the monarchy, constellations of bright stars gravitate around the face of the king, giving political pride of place to this form of valuation. But such a world can also be found in small American towns with their high school football stars and charismatic religious leaders, or in world cities where politicians or internationally recognized actors or politicians vie for the attention of sophisticated urbanites as they watch television or read newspapers online. It is not simply being a part of a social network linked to well-known people that makes this world but instead a sense that one might be more than any scheme of rational measure would account for. Here, as in a house of haute couture, the individual is always special, but some shine brighter than others, and those who shine the brightest attract followers and fans.

Maya's hanging on to her absent family and the absent circle of friends—thus enabling herself to recall other selves and other ways of judging people—leads me to think of Santosh, who explained that he would never move back to India because "family is butting in all the time and everything starts adding up." Even though he has moved to Dubai in part to enable his children to be more in touch with their Indian family, he seeks to elude the particular kind of family ties that Maya seems to embrace as a way of maintaining her own sense of an authentic self. Meanwhile, Majid's main gripe about his birthplace is that it encourages a form of inequality that is not just about measuring up, but of making oneself and one's possessions into something sacred, a sign of one's specialness, a pivot around which servants bow and with which to amaze one's friends. As he notes, the "good life" is a matter of the kinds of values one adopts; but as his own interpretation of a kind of abstraction that plagues Maya suggests, it is also a matter of balancing out coexisting goods. In following how women of all walks of life made decisions on apparently petty issues of style, I came to see that several worlds of experience and deliberation traverse the borders that are such a defining feature of migratory life. Might the very maps that enable serial migrants to tell their story be an obstacle to expressing some of their involvements in specific places? Might a model of different forms of social life that intersect everywhere, a model that takes into account the connection between who one is, how one meets others, and where one might travel, even within a city or neighborhood, illuminate some of the differences among the homelands where one might seek to become a particular kind of foreigner?

This interpretive schema leads me to clarify experimental aspects of serial migrant life. Because these worlds make up each of one's homelands in different measure, to move with these different worlds at one's disposition might offer a way of establishing a social continuity among one's homelands. One learns these worlds in commerce with others, but different political systems enable certain worlds to flourish, others to be diminished. Rather than imagining some singular nation or political or cultural system meeting the universal in a global ecumene, each person, organization, or state juggles coexisting worlds that have developed as a result of modern forms of art, knowledge, and sites of social interaction. Much like the serial migrant, states do not approach these worlds from afar, from some disengaged location; their history may inhibit certain choices or make certain worlds difficult to fit with others. Yet by directing where people go, by settling certain kinds of people in certain neighborhoods or cafés or homelands for a delimited or unlimited period, the state plays a major role in shaping how people associate with others and how they think. As we have seen, this does not mean that the state is the major force to be analyzed to get a sense of how paths intermingle to produce regional and global patterns, but it plays an essential role in ordering this ongoing dance.

Who gains access to places where one might learn these different ways of being together and that teach us how to engage in the constant process of judging the world? How might these coexisting worlds of value be related to one another in individual and collective experience? Who moves among these worlds, and how might those who have access to all three of them order them in their lives and thoughts? These are some of the questions that serial migrants implicitly address when they settle themselves in each new country.

Participating in proximate, celebrity, or fast places is a socialization into a way of understanding and evaluating the world at large. But because many of us participate in more than one kind of social setting, because we are involved in more than one world at once, points of passage among sites and situations when one worldview prevails become key moments in lives, and for analysis. For individuals, organizations, families, nations, or multinational corporations, knowing how and when and why to shift among worlds is a sign of social and political acumen. Serial migrants register their own continuities across homelands and in the process mark the distinct ways that different national political systems work with cross-national forms of life to promote a certain ordering of worlds, producing social differences and ethical and aesthetic dispositions in the process.

It is by noticing how markets and ideas, political entities and subjects are shaped by their participation or exclusion in these coexisting spaces of evaluation and action that we can begin to develop an understanding of how mobility shapes the globe in ways that are enmeshed with, but cannot be reduced to, questions of trajectory or connection. Subordinating or promoting one world or another is required to shape a powerful message or personality. Influence might be seen as being able to "pass" in situations where the criteria of each kind of social setting or "world" dominate. Interpreting how people explain their choices, hopes, or well-being in terms of the different social configurations of proximate, rational, and celebrity worlds of experience, one gets a sense of the way the serial migrant's experiment might reveal unimagined congruities among places of settlement or point out circumstances where a world run wild might not be sustainable.

In following the staccato rhythms of lives made up of border crossings, we should not lose sight of how individual direction arises neither through a singular imagination nor through a particular collective history, but through the ways we live with others and how different sites of settlement give value to these through political arrangements.[21] The homelands we have lived through promote distinct versions of collective life, conjugating ideals of society and modes of socialization by the way they facilitate or inhibit movements among worlds of experience that increasingly coexist in any single place even as they are scattered around the world.

When one comes to dwell on the particular kind of foreigner one might be in any place, taking on or into oneself the suspicion or curiosity of those who know only that they lack knowledge of the circumstances that have shaped one's modes of action and motives, one tends to locate ethical conundrums in these spaces of one's own absence to those who are now present. An ethics of invisibility might include considering how to represent oneself to those who are ignorant of the world arrangements that have shaped one's process of self-definition. To relinquish full communicability is not to let go of the possibility of expressive self-coherence. Certain places of settlement allow one to bring out this cohesiveness more fully because they favor one or another social and evaluative world. Different systems orient everyone to be most attuned to certain modes of social interaction, ideas, or projects. Similar, systematic ways of associating worlds may enable even the most immobile people to deliberate easily with one another across borders but may also cause them to take for granted that certain kinds of situations ought to call on particular forms of assessment. Noticing this might lead us to take a fressh approach to questions of ethnocentrism derived from assumptions about discrete cultural dispositions. The serial migrant's experience with alternative systems might heighten her appreciation or critique of this taken-for-grantedness the three-world model reveals. Even when she feels most at home, she is made of alternatives to the situation to which she feels most attuned. To explore this process of attunement requires further explanation of how ways of valuing relationships to others, to things, and to one's different selves evolve through serial migration. The way in which relationships to others might lead one to conceive of one's location and experiment as collective, the way in which others act as ciphers, enabling one to better understand one's sense of unfolding purpose, requires further consideration. From a poetics that leads us to notice that every homeland offers not simply histories but advice about the continuities of the body and imagination, it is time to question the fascination with space that characterizes recent decades and imagine a poetics of attachment.

CHAPTER 6

A POETICS OF ATTACHMENT

Sometimes the house of the future is better built, lighter and larger than all the houses of the past, so the image of the dream house is opposed to that of the childhood home. Late in life with indomitable courage, we continue to say that we are going to do what we have not yet done: we are going to build a house. . . . If these dreams are realized, they no longer belong in the domain of this study, but in that of the psychology of projects. However, as I have said many times, for me a project is short-range oneirism and while it gives free play to the mind, the soul does not find in it its vital expression. Maybe it is a good thing for us to keep a few dreams of a house that we shall live in later, always later, so much later, in fact, that we shall not have time to achieve it. For a house that was final, one that stood in symmetrical relation to the house we were born in, would lead to thoughts—serious, sad thoughts—and not to dreams. It is better to live in a state of impermanence than one of finality.[1]

IN *THE POETICS OF SPACE* Gaston Bachelard draws parallels between built structures and mental structures. His emphasis on dwellings' form enables us to grasp how a house—any house—can offer what he calls "counsels of continuity." The structural properties of a house are compelling because they elicit memories of past homes by comparison. We might notice how, along with our mental images of a roof, a window, or a staircase, our bodily gestures act as reminders of the past. When we enter a new home, we might at first take a wrong turn to find the bathroom, or notice how the height of the kitchen sink requires a different posture. Bachelard's psychoanalytic proclivities are apparent in his focus on the symbolic primacy of the house of childhood. The logic of his poetics, however, does not require any single home to dominate the poetics of space. He writes that our former homes "are never lost but live on in us," and that the house of the future is always "more beautiful" than those of the past.[2] What could be more true to a serial migrant, who, even if he never moves again, feels free only when he can imagine being able to move to a new home in a different homeland?

Although some have suggested that Bachelard is too obsessed with settlement, the house he sets out in his signature work appears on the horizon as a promise of shelter and protection in relation to the journey and the path.[3] His emphasis on "reverie" rather than dreaming opens up possibilities for the creative intervention of the subject in shaping her imaginative stance in ways that seem to me particularly suggestive in coming to terms with the often inchoate projects of serial migrants. The problem with Bachelard and phenomenology more generally is not a fixation with settlement but that his subject is so solitary.[4] Crossing the threshold of serial migrants' homes, I entered rooms full of noise and conversation. Talking with them of their daydreams, I recorded many versions of the fantasy with which I began this book, that of bringing together friends and relations from around the world. Inspecting their drawers and noticing what they carried with them in their suitcases, I saw that even the objects they chose to take with them everywhere were valued as symbols of affection. In contrast to Bachelard's image-filled rooms where one always sleeps alone, serial migrants' homes are often full of people. Individually, they move across the world for love. Collectively, they migrate to distance themselves from emotional situations that made them uncomfortable. They weave the evolving background of their lives with threads that bind them to particular others, leading me to imagine a poetics of attachment.[5]

For Nur, "home is where I have my Qur'an, my clothes, and where I keep my luggage." While her religiously inspired lack of concern for the house or homeland is unusual, the idea that the things one carries along in one's travels can create the space of one's life is not at all unusual. In home decor serial migrants often embrace a pared-down, modernist aesthetic. Whether this is due to some original disposition or the practical problems one encounters in moving things from country to country is impossible to know. The problem of accumulation that plagues serial migrants is mirrored in the winnowing of possessions that accompanies each displacement. Many of them express a sense of "lightness" when they get rid of old objects, but they also make a point of how the things they carry with them from one home to another are special. Indeed, like Nur's Qur'an, these things may be what makes any house a home. While some of these objects may be evidence of adherence to a belief system or an abstract "community," most are not. These chosen belongings tend to bear the imprint of some special person or act as conduits for evoking former selves or experiences.

NECESSARY OBJECTS

Although in most things Jamal conforms to a "less is more" aesthetic, he has never forsaken his collection of vinyl LPs. The record collection followed him as he moved from Fez to Toulouse to Rabat and then to Montreal. His family sold their autos and furniture and gave away loads of clothing and household items with each move, because without institutional support they needed to limit costs. But Jamal always found a way to come up with extra cash to ship his fragile assortment of albums. In each place he saved up to acquire a top-quality stereo system. He has an impressive set of CDs as well, but like many connoisseurs he prefers the sound quality of records. Some of the LPs have gained in market value over time, but this is not his concern. Their value emerges from the poetic functions they fulfill. A guitar riff makes Jamal that teenager in Fez—right here, right now. It might lead him to recall the young man who traveled to England to ask for Leila's hand. Some melodies make him wonder what life would be like today had he continued working in a psychiatric hospital in Toulouse and lived out his life as an immigrant in France.

In 2005 Jamal got out his records as we drank champagne to celebrate his wedding anniversary. Leila and I danced beside the table; the children and their friends watched us and laughed. In 2007 we met again, this time at Floresca's house in London. Jamal's records were back in Canada, but we could listen to them because Floresca had copies of the same songs (unfortunately on CDs—oh, well!). London was where Leila and Floresca first met decades ago, where they had heard some of these airs together as young women. The England they experienced then was surely very different from the England I called home at the time of our meeting in that North London living room— the England I would soon be leaving for my fourth migration to the United States—but the music provided a way of connecting those times and imaginatively adding to them.

I have suggested that while the serial migrant's very definition overemphasizes the state, our subjective continuity is enabled by ideational and ethical worlds that cross borders, worlds that evolve through specific forms of interaction with others that are increasingly universal. One might imagine that like the continuities of Bachelard's house, these social and judgmental circles, grids, and constellations might offer a sense of comfort, a chance to feel at ease in new circumstances, but also a way of examining the changes in oneself and one's truths. A life of progressive settlements might offer opportunities for moving into or out of world arrangements one finds problematic. When Jamal sets the needle on the grooves of the very record he purchased in the medina decades ago, when he touches the very same disc with the very same movement of his wrist, he affirms the self by reference to gestures and airs that are collective: music moves among social worlds, ignores borders, draws us together in the present, recalls individual performers, their voices ever youthful. Memories and present sensations are drawn out by the music, which can prompt shared emotion that might recall *communitas*; but there is no congregation, even if there may very well be a sense of expressive fulfillment. A song makes the past present, connects Jamal to a generation, and offers the potential for reanimating this history collectively with old friends or people he has just met. Intimacy and performance, public and personal history, the possibility of taking a life forward—this special mass-produced object enables all of this.

We who danced in Montreal and London might appear to be a cosmopolitan assortment of friends who share a global culture: individuals originally from Greece, Morocco, Ireland, and the United States, listening to songs in English while speaking mainly French, representatives of an emerging world consciousness that many say is most apparent in elite networks and global cities. Yet more precise commonalities were also apparent: we shared very specific memories of being with these very people. Seeing people we cared about together for the first time might be a joyful incarnation of the reverie of bringing *all* of our loved ones together. The music was a medium for reveling in a poetics of attachment that was very specific to each subject, not simply some generalized appeal to a global youth culture in the course of growing old. One does not rejoice in the generalities of being a cosmopolitan. The songs that Jamal carries with him do not speak of a desire for recognition in general, from the world, but instead express a yearning to find oneself reflected in the eyes of the beloved.

THE SPECIAL OTHER

Maya and Nick, Evelyn and Alex, among many others, urged me to consider the idea that one may travel as an individual motivated by a desire to define oneself, but one always settles because of someone else. They were unanimous and emphatic in their conviction that without the mention of love no account of migratory desire could be accurate or complete. A *coup de foudre* can offer a glimpse of the fulfillment one seeks in the eyes of the beloved; an *Augenblick* shapes the development of the serial migrant's narrative in a search for meaning.[6] The "apocalypse" of love, like the ecstasy of art, is not merely a reverie but a potential for creation. When it leads to an ongoing commitment, individuals not only collaborate to explore the world together, they also move through the society of others as a collective subject.

One might suppose that just as the serial migrant progresses through selves, one after another, to weave a lifeline, he might easily shrug off relationships as he moves on, embracing a solitary ideal. Considering the misunderstandings he lives through everywhere, one might think he would become secretive, carefully policing his exchanges with others so as to limit situations where misrecognition leads to discomfort. It would not be unreasonable for the serial migrant to develop a certain reserve, thus discouraging others from asking questions that he would find it difficult to answer. Presenting oneself to others in such a calculated manner might sound like a way of eluding the truth about oneself. A life path that involves renouncing the ideal of a transparent fullness of communication and embraces diverse truths about the self might seem simply insincere or contradictory.[7] One might again expect to find in the serial migrant a cold cosmopolitan distance or a nomadic self-reliance. Yet just as moves cause someone to reassess her possessions and reaffirm her affection for special things, they can also redefine, stretch, and intensify relationships to others. Attachments to people and places are not easy to disentangle.

Some people "fall in love with a place through a person" or vice versa, Evelyn told me. Although she and her Egyptian fiancé split up before marrying, it was through the warm embrace of his family that she came to feel firmly connected to Egypt. Indeed, she remains in touch with them many years later. The lover, the friend, or the sister-in-law becomes a conduit to a new kind of involvement in one's environment, in this case amplifying one's depth of experience of proximate worlds with their collective judgments, which can often be a source of support for the individual.[8] Sometimes such relationships are brief: the object of one's fascination is alluring at first because he enables one to explore the new environment; he becomes less interesting once one knows one's way around. Many of my interlocutors looked at such relationships as frivolous, perhaps even unworthy of mention in the story of a life. Some pointed out that "using" another simply as a tool in one's individual experiment with self did not fit their ideals of a "pure" relationship. Yet many of these relationships lasted for a long period of time; some led to marriage. Even some who married "for papers" usually made a point of explaining that they did not enter the relationship with the simple goal of obtaining a long-term visa or passport. Just as most serial migrants resist an accounting of themselves in terms of career goals and capital accumulation, they do not generally see personal relationships as a route to enhancing their citizenship potential or economic position, or as the successful culmination of their "scientific" experiment with each new site.

Sometimes a love affair with a person who has never left his or her birthplace leads the serial migrant to settle indefinitely. But in many of the stories I recorded, the new couple decided to move on; the person who had seemed sedentary longed to travel, perhaps enraptured by the other's apparent ease of motion. In this situation the one who was already an immigrant, perhaps a serial migrant, relives her own initiation through the rite of passage of another. She might be considered a mentor in migration in a process that leads to the conception of a collective migratory subject. This subject is complex; not only does each individual face new truths in each new home, but each partner envisions these differently according to his or her migratory path. The rite of passage of first immigration is a transformative experience. One might then suffer the push and pull between first and second homelands; one might generalize about the world at large in the dual terms typical of immigration. This can be difficult for the partner who is becoming a serial migrant or has already settled in multiple countries. Differences can emerge not only in response to the homeland at hand, but also in the way one's migratory identity shapes one's relation to every landscape, one's way of being a foreigner. To live migration again with a first-time immigrant might lead to a renewal of one's own story through the birth or further development of the new collective migratory subject.

A border-crossing life might encourage reflections on the implications of various forms of self-renunciation, critically engaging the idea that one might ever be fully present to anyone, exploring how particular relationships or situations enable certain "you's" to become apparent. However, a situation of differential migratory experience can lead to such a setting aside of so much of what drives one's internal conversation that the fulfillment one seeks in the other may be endangered; love might die even while a relationship persists. The stories I have collected suggest that serial migrants may be more inclined than other people to put an end to this kind of situation by moving elsewhere, marking a change in the storyline.

Migratory experience is not everything; many couples mismatched in migration have much else in common. But one should not underestimate the difference made by the path of migration. It is striking how many couples seem to find a solution by seeking what one might call migratory parity, by moving on to some further point of settlement and thus both becoming serial migrants. The move seems to create a more equal collaboration, a joint effort to develop a collective history and to seek fulfillment in one's partner.

Very few of the border-crossing people I encountered had been with the same partner from the beginning of their migration story. Even those who shared a birth country often met when they were both immigrants in a second homeland. As we have seen, the second homeland can overtake the first as a point of reference; this phenomenon seems more common among those who meet their spouse-to-be during this interval. Even for those who hear the trace of a long history of serial migration in each other's voices, the place they are settled when they first encounter one another becomes a departure for the story of the newly formed subject.

Relationships often encounter bureaucratic obstacles for those who move from one country to another. Those who are individually recruited on set term contracts are often granted individual visas only. Moves made without papers are often expected to lead to a reunion with the loved one, but the barriers are often insurmountable and couples live apart for very long periods of time. Gay couples face special difficulties settling together in a new country, but even a marriage certificate for a heterosexual couple is no guarantee that residence will be approved for both partners.

A number of the individuals I followed for this study attribute their inability to find a partner to the legal restrictions of their pattern of settlement. Although Maria has had a couple of boyfriends, getting married and having children would put a stop to her successive jobs in various countries. Unless she met someone from a place where she might acquire residency papers, not being able to work would mean returning to the Philippines, which she does not want to do. The segregation of people according to nationality and function in the Gulf means that she has little chance of meeting someone who might lead her to settle in some further country. She socializes mainly with other women who are also domestic workers, shying away from men since a terrifying encounter when she barely escaped rape; she did suffer physical assault because she refused sexual favors. That encounter with a "local" led her to abandon any romantic ideas she might have had about the possibility of a relationship that could enable her to settle where she lives at present. Perhaps her next contract will take her somewhere else, she muses, somewhere like the United States or Australia. She seems to project her own dreams when she tells me of her friend Lily, who worked for years for various families in Europe and the Gulf and then ended up marrying an American, having a daughter, and moving to Texas.

Several of the young unmarried or recently divorced men and women who did not have children said they looked forward to meeting a person with whom they might start a family. These young people in their twenties or early thirties tended to be very "settled" in their images of their future family. As the preceding chapters have amply documented, however, marriage and children are often a reason for moving, either for a certain period of time or for a yet-to-be-determined interval. Several women, such as Rheinhilde, did arrest their desire to move on until their children were out of school, and others, such as Noha, envisage a time when their children will be adults as something to look forward to, a time when they will be able to move again if they choose. In contrast, Kamala left her three children in India with her husband when she worked in Dubai for a few years and then when she settled in Qatar, where she was able to set up her own shop and gain long-term residence. Her daughter had just turned eighteen and completed high school, and was thus able to fulfill the requirements for a work visa. Now Mohindi and her daughter work together, making frequent visits to India to see the rest of the family. Couples and families work on the "experimental" aspect of migration together, unfolding a shared location that might include disparate sites simultaneously. This can add to the sense of a collective fulfillment and identity, but it also presents challenges.

TIES

Each move of any individual might upset, define, or redefine a couple or a family. Moves to new homes often challenge what a couple is, or who counts as a family member, in ways that displacement within a particular homeland does not. Resettlement can be a chance to test the nature of one's attachments. Repeated immigration might emphasize the particularity of the collective subject, lessening the need for recognition from others outside the family circle. The couple or family might evolve in a home environment that becomes increasingly separate from the world at large, as though the individual household mimics the ethnic enclave, even when its members are of different national origins. Nonetheless, possibilities for such enclosure differ depending on where one is living. Noha's attention to the different styles of being a foreigner is also a matter of concern for the collective subject.

Collective migratory subjects must adapt to often complex circumstances, as is perhaps most apparent when they inhabit different countries simultaneously. But even when they are able to move together, a new homeland means changes for each individual—an alteration in status or occupation, the need to develop new language skills, and the evolution of how one is identified according to ethnic, class, or racial characteristics. As the individual evolves, the collective subject must adjust. We might recall that Santosh comments that, in India, "family" is always butting in. Proximate inequalities defined by kinship absorb the couple and their children into a larger family circle, and there are no scruples about judging all manner of things one decides for one's children. Indeed, not to put in one's "two cents" would be to abdicate one's family responsibilities. Catherine, in contrast, finds it problematic that the nuclear family is so enclosed in North America. She says the arrangement knots parents and children so tightly together that it is difficult for the adults to have a "full social life outside of work and the children's activities"; there is "way too much pressure on just the two of us." The system works against the egalitarian and individualistic values she sought when she moved to the United States, and she is thinking it might be best for the marriage if they all decided to move again, perhaps to a European city.

The composition of the family and how different individuals may be included in it is part of many of the collective reflections of the serial migrants I followed. On one hand, one may, like Majid, choose a place to settle on the basis of how its political organization favors a certain world, a particular way of promoting the values one hopes to emphasize in one's life and the education of one's children. But there are tradeoffs, since one is also seeking a particular kind of family relationship. The question is not merely what kind of person one seeks to become or hopes one's children will become, but how kin might interact. One might decide, like Akhil and his wife, to live in a country that permits a close connection to the extended family due to geographical proximity. Like Santosh, they want their children to develop relationships with their cousins in India. Why then do they live in Qatar? one might ask, especially since Akhil makes no secret of his disdain for a political system that promotes blatant inequalities; recall his attempts to visit Indian laborers to "help them out." Still, he reasons, although there are many things about Qatar that he does not like, it is a site from which his family can more easily connect with kin without the problem Santosh described, of family "butting in." Akhil seeks to encourage individual relationships between his children and their cousins, but without becoming entangled in a world of proximity that would enable the extended family to chime in on each decision he and his wife make about their daughter's clothing or their son's education. Although the kind of one-on-one relationship he favors might be associated with rational worlds that assume equality among individuals, worlds that do not prevail in Qatari political or social life, living there offers certain private advantages for the present. These are not easily explained according to a desire for financial gain or the selection of a preferred political system; rather, they have to do with developing family relationships, getting a little closer to family for a set period of the children's lives while also retaining a comfortable or productive distance.

It is not surprising that for people who consider countries the markers for times in their lives, places are summed up in terms of particular people who have played a role in shaping their life story, even in their absence making it an evolving part of their narrative and themselves. One might recall a house with nostalgia, but the feelings of joy or melancholy associated with it have much to do with memories of particular people enclosed within its walls, some of whom will stay there forever, lost to the dreamer, perhaps because they have passed away or perhaps because they have been left behind by the forward motion of a life, sometimes by choice, sometimes by a lack of attentiveness.

Serial migrants say overwhelmingly that they make friends of others who have similar experiences of displacement, of settling in, of readjusting attachments to others with each move. But they also maintain connections with the homelands they have left through people they came to know there. Vincenza's second homeland was Czechoslovakia, a country that has been divided and thus is no longer. The communist system she applauded, which gave her a life that made her unconcerned with material things, is now long since dissolved. Yet over all of the years since she left, she has maintained a friendship with her old roommate: the person who—unlike her first roommate in the graduate school dorm—did not ask her if people in Africa lived in trees, the friend who accompanied her on picnics in the country with their boyfriends. She wants to bring her daughter, who is growing up in London, to visit Prague; seeing Prague will be nice, but it is really her friend that she wants to see; she should have kept up more, wanted to be more in touch. A visit would be just the thing to reanimate not only their relationship but also a memory of a location that cannot be evoked simply by touring the buildings of a changing city. A tie to a person is not only an evocation of a place that may no longer exist on the map, but a substantiation of one's ongoing relationship to what one made of oneself through life with that other person in that place, and one's ongoing reliance on them.

Abdelwahab is a serial migrant presently living in Canada with his wife and children. When Leila asked him if he had any advice for people who might follow in his migratory footsteps, he said he did: he would tell them to move with the idea that they could not possibly change their mind; once they had decided they should settle in a new place, they needed to stick with the decision. "If you take the straight road and follow it, if your aim is clear, if you are direct, you win, that's for sure. . . . A second very important thing is that you must live as things present themselves here, be happy with the day-to-day life, think you are better here than anywhere else." His experience of several migrations has led him to see the futility of thinking about what one lacks in terms of some other place. That leads to "stagnation." To keep up with one's own life is not to forget, however. "Keep your ties to those elsewhere," he urges the prospective migrant. This may be a way of hedging one's bets. What if one needed to return to where one lived previously? Who would one count on? But perceiving the ties to others in material terms is inadequate. When networks and connections are taken for granted, we miss the fact that the "straight road" to settlement is not a path well worn by people with a common context; rather, it is a path made by those whose attachments to particular others enable them to become clearer about themselves and about the worlds they inhabit or the world arrangements they reject.

The value of motion is not easy to measure; the loss of oneself that might accompany moving to yet one more place is easy to recognize. Yet, the advantages of repeated settlement are perhaps less apparent. The way a room might offer counsel that is pertinent only when a song once heard is played again; a form of life that makes a ritual of displacement in which a liminal moment shows the friend's face that is the homeland or one's own face made up as a particular kind of foreigner, whose stories evolve through state lines, but decisions entail reflections on social worlds pictured as circles, grids or constellations, people deliberating differently to ask the same questions, observing the world and coming up with solutions in terms of these worlds, but also seeing what happens when the values of one world are imported into another; passing among homes, settling in, moving among political systems that work with world passages to push habits one can't leave behind, addictions that leave little room for free motion or thought, or to lead us to engage certain manners of relating to others. A poetics is made of the stuff of experience, but it escapes from the bounds of history, ignoring chronology to notice how deliberation has shaped the whole as an intimation of movement toward meaning, desire, the discipline of style.

I found myself daydreaming about what it would be like to be one of those cherished objects one could not leave behind:

> I traveled widely. I moved as if no wide expanse of water, no soundless sea of words, might still that forward motion upon which life thrives. In drawing close what seemed distant my charms increased with each caress, each man or woman or place enhanced by my custody, because I bore the mark of every passage lightly. I was the magic that passed from hand to hand, the Kula shell that rubbed your palms to carry along your trace to others you could not imagine, each partaking in what value I acquired through others, the dream of what I would next become to someone else somewhere else.

I imagined the anthropologist in the image of the kula shell:

> What would happen if the anthropologist were no longer the careful designer of collaborative projects or a complicitous fellow traveler, but instead an object of circulation and barter among those who keep her for a certain time and then pass her on? What would be her version of the time spent in the islands of an archipelago that cannot be sketched on any map because its countries are made of the chapters of a story of settlement?

And I wrote of myself:

> Je suis traversée par des paysages divers,
> Par des langages étrangères les unes aux autres.
> Je suis éparpillée par les vents et les vagues,
> Par des nuages opaques qui voilent mon visage.
> Il n'y a que toi qui me ramasse et me rassemble
> Tes yeux, le miroir qui montre un monde qui me ressemble.

I am traversed by diverse landscapes,
By languages foreign to one another.
I am scattered by the wind and the waves,
Opaque clouds veil my face.
Only you gather me up and put me together,
Your eyes the reflection of a world that resembles me.

And finally:

Sunday morning brings a reverie,
Your hands knotting ropes to set sail.
Tying knots tightly to gather momentum
You move a line low, then high
Adjusting attachments and fixations
To gather the breeze and navigate,
Stitching water to land, Earth to sky.

CONCLUSION

I N FOLLOWING those who have stepped beyond a single immigration, I have had to leave behind dreams of cosmopolitan distance from the earth, to forsake a politics of direct action in order to make sense of the experience that leads some people to use borders to mark intervals in their lives. In setting out in the company of the serial migrant, I have been taken to locations where the solid ground of social thought gives way, where experience has shown me the futility of appeals to reground theory while making me question why one might celebrate mobility for its own sake. Listening to serial migrants search for words while observing the pathways they refuse to take has led me to seek a more precise diagnostic than is possible if one simply marvels at our motion across the world or the way our circulation precedes or follows that of things or ideas. In exploring our settlements and how they incite us to embark on journeys with destinations that are unclear even to ourselves, I have had to consider our resemblance to states that engage in ironic uses of their territories, displacing the ideal of peoples inhabiting landscapes bequeathed to them by history to create strategic alliances, playing on the myths of modern politics to leave migrants to make themselves of outdated maps.

When thoughts about the future are conceived as possible thanks to critical distance, we can easily fail to notice how mobility can favor the maintenance of old maps and worn-out notions of culture might hold some people in place with what might be called overidentification, while what is most essential to others' efforts to live beautiful or ethical or simply coherent lives goes unrecognized. Inequalities among serial migrants arise because of the passports they hold, and yet their stories show that for even the least endowed in citizenship, borders can act not only as barriers and enclosures but also as dream catchers. To travel across them is to notice consistencies of social life that point to the way states seek to conjugate social worlds systematically, favoring certain forms of movement and styles of settlement as part of their striving to consolidate themselves, their work with space and image and the land conceived through strategic alliances with one another. What one might call the politics of direction is not only a matter of international migration; it is at work in practices of sequestration and exile, in the way illiteracy or gender inequality or ethnic bias confine or expand one's range of motion or one's ability to join in collective deliberations, and forms of self. I have suggested that by concentrating on the movement instead of the classifications or confinements it produces as race or class or gender, we might recognize commonalities among people who might otherwise seem profoundly different, separated by that very striating work of the state that cannot be challenged by any nomadic formation, because states are themselves conceived in terms of projects that do not honor the definition given them by international politics.

From thinking about how politics might address the foreigner in our midst, or studying how these others develop themselves in some transnational space or diasporic cloud, consideration of the kind of foreigner one might be becomes emblematic of an emerging politics. States as well as individuals evolve in a dance that one cannot observe all at once, but this does not preclude gaining an understanding of their operations.

Closer inspection of the way the dance of settlement and mobilization enables or inhibits possibilities for collective action or creativity is surely in order: I have only barely sketched out how this project might be carried forward. Some might be surprised that my subjects do not marvel at the wonders of time/space compression, the way that electronic communications and cheaper transportation have made the world smaller. Some might protest that I have focused not on connectivity but on attachments, wisps of affection and questions of memory tied to place through particular people; I have left to the reader's imagination much of how the serial migrant's motion relates to a more general dance of politics, society, and culture. One would need to explore further the cadence and direction of other ways of moving through the world to take this step. One would also need to examine the way state interventions lead subjects who have set out on varied routes to meet under particular circumstances, but even then one might develop some equation that explains the generation of particular political and social formations without mapping the whole; the global world this approach might describe is not scalar. Breaking with the spatial obsessions that have characterized recent decades does not imply speeding up the chase to overtake light waves, but patiently working through the specific ways that the warm embrace that is the society of others is not opposed to but part of the kinds of processes that have been considered so alienating in discourses of modernity and globalization. Moving to understand serial migrants' stories distances me from the way that migration has been studied as the encounter of a constituted social body with the stranger and nudges me toward a poetics of attachments that might include further investigation of the powers that push some people to move, others to stay, and all of us to ponder the way that mobility can make certain things or subjects valuable or invisible.

By carefully following how displacement produces distinctive possibilities for dwelling with others and forming attachments to people, objects, or guitar riffs, we might not immediately arrive at the generality expressed in cosmopolitan dreams for world peace. We might, however, come closer to finding out how the world picture is progressively made by movements that incorporate long-received ideas about social and political life. Further research on states' modes of operation and the work of corporations is surely in order; the relative lack of primarily economically determined goals among many of those I write of—those who might be expected to reap the benefit of an increasingly integrated world economy—needs further investigation. Could it be that politics is reasserting itself? That the ethical ideals of collective life I have discussed in terms of the interplay of proximate, rational, and celebrity worlds is perhaps essential to the play of global corporations, that serial migrants' reflections on modes of state operation may actually prefigure the strategies of economically conceived actors? Traveling in the company of serial migrants might be initially perceived as an effort to record their life stories as epics of the network society or evidence of the contradictions of neo-liberalism. But closer acquaintance suggests that to do so would be not only presumptuous but distract us from what they can actually teach us about emerging forms of social difference that are inherently political and that are essential in determining how value is bestowed and exchange carried out.

As I conclude this try, this trial, this test at making a path through the world an object of reflection, I remark the extent to which this essay follows Abdelwahab's advice to potential migrants to "take the straight road and follow it." A certain reserve and severity of expression, a stubbornness of analytic direction apparent in these pages, might serve as yet another example of the austere aesthetic that repeated settlement encourages. One might protest the lack of illustrative materials that would have been included had I approached my subjects as splendid assemblages, or dwelt on their marvelous variety of cultural or national or class origins. Yet this attempt to develop an anthropological account of a form of life where ethnos is not absent but no longer definitional, this effort to describe an unfolding search that finds its location in a process of progressive evaluation enabled by selves made with respect to old maps and reified political and cultural systems, required close attention to a common path. The lives of the people I encountered for this work are so full of significant detail that they themselves are often overwhelmed by their wealth of experience. They alone will be able to decide whether my focus on form to explain our lives might enable a positive diagnostic, perhaps even a cure for what ails us. As for those who have taken different paths and settled otherwise, I hope that this account of serial migration might offer some ideas about how their stories might be told. Then, a more comprehensive understanding of the evolving politics of movement might be possible.

REFERENCE MATTER

NOTES

INTRODUCTION

1. The most influential typologies are those of Hannerz 1996 (original 1990) and Clifford 1997.

2. The term "serial migration" has been used by some other writers to describe the way that individuals of a single group progressively follow one another from their place of origin to a second homeland, a kind of relay in a network of ethnicity and family or nationality. In this sense serial migration is an equivalent term for "chain migration." Its unit of analysis is often the family unit or an ethnic group; its "seriality" consists of individuals who follow in the path of others in this group who previously immigrated to a common host country. It was not in reaction to this line of work but with reference to the importance of the serial logic of the subjects I set out to follow that I came to adopt this term (Ossman 2004). I was gratified that many of those I met in the course of this research were thrilled to learn that my project gave them a name, put words to something they felt but for which they had found no words in any of the places they had lived. I had worried that the uncouth title I had given this project would perhaps dissuade some people from participating, yet I could not think of any more accurate way to describe it. However, rather than rejecting a term associated with other forms of iteration that are figured as deeply negative, like the "serial killer," or perhaps regrettable, such as "serial monogamy," many of those I encountered in the course of this research expressed an audible sigh of relief when I offered to include them in this

designation. I also refer to the subjects of my study in this book in other terms to lighten the burden of reading; terms such as "cross-country people," "border-crossing people," "those who have made repeated migrations," and others will be readily understood as equivalent to "serial migrants."

3. One thinks of Homi Bhabha's conception of the third space of immigration as a creative breaking in of the foreign (Bhabha 1994). I have previously suggested that configuration is problematic because it takes for granted the lack of strangeness to itself of the host society (Ossman 2002, pp. 156–57).

4. For the tendency to take "discrete, bounded groups as chief constituents in social life, chief protagonists of social conflicts, and fundamental units of social analysis," Rogers Brubaker uses the term "groupism" (Brubaker 2006, p. 8).

5. Faubion 2001, p. xiv.

6. Oakeshott 1995, p. 91.

7. The practice of assemblage is associated with artists ranging from Pablo Picasso to Marcel Duchamps and Jean Dubuffet. Many scholars have recently adopted the term to discuss the heterogeneous "assemblages" that life forms and social processes, not to mention research designs and methods, take on in a situation of globalization. Thus, in Collier and Ong's impressive collection of articles on globalization, the editors write that this work "suggests no unified theoretical approach," just as they suggest that globalization is made of "several logics" (Ong and Collier 2005, 16). While one cannot but agree with their ideas about the lack of isomorphism of the "standard units of analysis" and the phenomena that concern "social scientists" is a problem, we would do well to be cautious about the limits of a logic of assemblage (ibid., p. 3). Serial migrants struggle with the conceptual problems inherent in "assemblage." In conceiving of this project and examining their stories I start by noting the ruptures of serial migrant life as they tell it, sticking with "standard units of analysis" in keeping with the native categories of those whose form of life I am trying to understand. Only after that do they delve into the description of the "several logics" that they engage everywhere.

For other influential uses of assemblage in explorations of social intercourse and globalization, see Latour 2005 and Sassen 2006. For an early and incisive analysis of the way in which that modernist collage and "assemblage" came to be taken as models for ethnographic writing see Marcus 1998.

8. Thus, this approach differs from the kind of accumulation that Aihwa Ong signaled in her work on flexible citizens. She critiques Bourdieu's "relatively

homogeneous and static fashion" of treating symbolic capital, noting that her subjects must consider "sets of competing cultural criteria" and that North American and European styles are dominant (Ong 1988, pp. 91–93).

I agree with those who suggest that it is not "North American and European" style but modern forms more generally that ought to be taken into account. Competing cultural criteria must be seen as related to modern forms of knowledge and self-formation that are not as singular or perhaps as "Western" as some have suggested (see, for example, Taylor 1989). In the present work I write of accumulation as it relates to the systematic way that my subjects evaluate systems and the selves they might produce, the often tiny shifts in meaning that the subject notes as she moves from one state system to another, differences that are not easily portrayed in terms of easy hierarchies of models. The additions and accretions that my subjects seem most concerned with are related to discourses of hyphenation and hybridity, themselves indicative of the unsustainability of many received ideas about how social and political life hang together.

9. We live in an epoch when the "new rules of the political game make it more difficult to define the relation between what who is, what one can do and what one is supposed to accomplish," as Foucault wrote of politics and relationships to the self in the fading Roman Empire (Foucault 1984, p. 105, my translation). By working through the serial migrant's moves to bring different histories together, I proceed in a way that makes it difficult to theorize about changing subjects in terms of any shared background, however complex and changing. In contrast to those who would "reground" or resituate theory, perhaps because the post-modern turn has passed, as Adele Clarke would have it, I use a method that is expected to provide "ground knowledge" for theorization toward an increasingly "ungrounded" relationship of the subject with her environment. This follows the lead of authors who have suggested the need for a profound reformulation of ethnographic location and practice (Coleman and Collins 2006; Gingrich and Fox 2002; Gupta and Ferguson 1997; Marcus 1998, 2007; Rabinow et al. 2008).

10. This project began to take shape in late 2001. In the days and months after 9/11 the media highlighted the chameleon character of the terrorists (Ossman 2004, 2007a). Accounts of the vodka-drinking Mohammed Atta filled newspapers, while the sanity of Zacarias Moussaoui was discussed in terms of his moves among several countries in his youth (Terrio 2007). Multiple displacements across the world can make someone an object of suspicion, despite the fact that global labor markets, NGOs, and international organizations increasingly need individuals

who pass easily across borders. In the classroom I am expected to teach tolerance, encourage students to study foreign languages and to become familiar with "other" cultures. My own experience of serial migration and research seems to make me ideally suited to teach others how to slide easily across boundaries; yet, as someone whose fieldwork has been largely in the Arab world, I felt also that questions about my motives led some to find new "explanations" of this engagement ("Now I see why you spent all of that time studying this stuff—now I get the importance," one longtime acquaintance told me in October 2001) and to harbor suspicions of my association with the changelings who had attacked us (Ossman 2007a). We often complain about how anthropologists tend to become overly concerned with representing "their" people, or presumptuous in "giving voice" to those they study, but one might also note that they are often assumed to take on some of the attributes of those they study by a sort of contagion. In any event, the kinds of complicities and identifications that fieldwork can entail must be reconsidered at a time when control is increasingly shifted from the kinds of gestures and commonalities studied by classical fieldwork to the recording of subjects' digital trails and the registering of the shapes of their irises.

11. I was born in the USA and lived in France for many years.

12. Ossman 2007b.

13. Barry Mirkin notes: "Among the Gulf Cooperation Council Countries, the proportion of foreign-born ranges from 30 percent to almost 90 percent. By comparison, one of the countries with the highest proportions of foreign-born residents in Europe is Switzerland, where the proportion foreign-born is some 23 percent of the population. Among cities where migrants are generally concentrated, such as Montreal, New York and Toronto, the foreign-born represent about one-third of the population" (Mirkin 2010, p. 27).

14. Early 2007 argues that one might be successively and simultaneously a serial migrant and a diplomat. Much of what I recount in the coming pages may resonate with anyone who has lived in a number of countries or cities or even moved from one house to another. I defined the subject of this study in such a way as to place attention on heightening the stakes of such displacements because they might thus better illuminate some of the dilemmas faced by everyone seeking to move into a new home or homeland. As I will explain, my research has emphasized the importance of moving through immigration for the formation of this subject. Not all of those who dwell in a succession of homes or homelands have the same stake in settling in; nor do they suffer the same losses of self-recognition or tempt fortune in the same manner.

15. Interviewees gave written or oral consent following an explanation of the aims of this research. Those who selected not to use their own names selected their own pseudonyms. I did not ask about their legal status, but several spoke freely about the changes in their status in the course of their histories.

16. Once, a junior year abroad was considered to be for a few adventurous foreign-language majors. According to the Institute of International Education, "Study abroad by students enrolled in U.S. higher education has more than tripled over the past two decades" (http://www.iie.org/en/Who-We-Are/News-and-Events/Press-Center/Press-Releases/2011/2011-11-14-Open-Doors-Study-Abroad).

17. See Beck 2006 and my critique, Ossman 2006.

18. See, for instance, Sayad 1999.

19. On the doubling of self by the market, see Marcus 1995.

20. There is a literalness in this project of "Oneself as Another" that, while concerned with self-narrative following Ricoeur, offers a very different approach from his to explain what social worlds intervene to shape how the self might show concern for the other (Ricoeur 1992). The subject is a form, as Foucault explains, but a form that is made of public worlds that are themselves not simply changing or indistinct, but different for each serial migrant (Foucault 1984, p. 290).

21. For more on emplotment see Ricoeur 1984, 1985, 1988, and White 1999.

22. For the initial formulation, see Ossman 2004.

23. This is not to say that economic factors are unimportant, but one might also notice how certain explorations of neo-liberalism tend to be projected as a uniform background against which to view individual actions or desires. For more on "exceptions" to neo-liberalism, see Ong 2006. Serial migrants sometimes choose to opt out of the very idea of accrual of capital as a life value in part because the labor market and measures of educational attainment are not universal; it is often very difficult to convert one's degrees or experience from one country to another, and of course arriving in a new place with few or no personal connections can make it difficult to enter many professional milieux, even when one is technically qualified. See Chapter 5.

24. Serial migrants trace their movements across standard world maps to set out the periods of their life. They develop a progressive life history by an ongoing displacement of themselves as they "are" in one of their countries into the next. A process of "emplotment" is facilitated by reference to identities, categorical labels, and world maps as they relate to the subject, who makes herself in the midst of these and by associating them in a certain order. Hayden White explores the tropic possibilities of displacements in terms of different genres of historical

writing. I draw on his work to ask how different problems arise when one's story is woven not in the fairly homogeneous "contexts" he assumes to offer the background to the historian, but across places that themselves include tropic displacements of what might constitute a state, a people, or a kind of person (White 1999, p. 8).

25. Caroline Brettel writes: "Martin et al. (2006) have suggested that if the world's migrants were gathered as one 'nation' it would be the sixth most populous. This astounding fact, in and of itself, is a call to anthropologists to place the global 'nation' of migrants at the forefront of their research agenda" (Brettell 2007, pp. 47–59). For recent statistics and an overview on global migration trends, see Goldin et al. 2011.

26. Francastel 1983.

CHAPTER I

1. For an extremely helpful overview of the literature, see Beck and Sznaider 2010. Academic definitions of the cosmopolitan have tended to contrast the cosmopolitan's mobility against the background of the local (Beck 2001; Hannerz 1996). Although the cosmopolitan's journey toward generality is usually told in a lighthearted, lively manner, the tales of refugees or exiles are recounted in dramatic and decidedly tragic colors. These different modes of narration participate in a trope that has dominated discussions about mobility and settlement as they relate to social position and progress since the Enlightenment.

2. Popular images tend to present the cosmopolitan as eminently cool, whether in the sense of being always in control, in sync with changing fashions, or unflappable in situations of disaster, famine, or upheaval. One often finds this unflappable figure set against backgrounds that suggest that he is globally mobile, conflating his image with the earlier picture of the "jet setter." The title of the popular magazine *Cosmopolitan* joins the idea of travel to discourses about the sexual connotations of feminine mobility.

3. Simmel in Frisby and Featherstone 1987, pp. 149–50.

4. Craig Calhoun has written that "cosmopolitans often fail to recognize the social conditions of their own discourse, presenting it as a freedom from social belonging rather than a special sort of belonging" (Calhoun 2003, p. 532). He argues that "solidarity" still matters. But many writers who have embraced the cosmopolitan actually pay close attention to the relationship of the cosmopolitan subjects they discuss and the legitimate claims of "nations, ethnicities, local communities, or religions" that he is afraid are being left aside (ibid.). It seems

to me that many of those engaged in fleshing out the cosmopolitan are in fact extremely interested in the relationship of the way the becoming-cosmopolitan is related to these claims—either as the basis in terms of the kinds of rights that might be recognized in a cosmopolitan political order for individual becoming-cosmopolitan. I interpret the "distancing" involved in this kind of becoming as too general to catch the various manners of taking distance related to different experiences of mobility.

5. Bronislaw Szerszynski and John Urry have suggested that three kinds of travel are particularly significant in creating the conditions for a cosmopolitan mode of being in the world: physical, bodily travel, which has become a way of life for many in Western societies; imaginative travel, to be transported elsewhere through the images and places and peoples encountered in the media; and virtual travel, transcending geographical and often social distance through information and communications technology (Szerszynski and Urry 2006, p. 115; also see Urry 2000).

6. Turner suggests that "cosmopolitan virtue" involves a distancing related to modes of Socratic irony (Turner 2002).

7. For some examples see Lamont and Aksartova 2002 on "ordinary cosmopolitanism" and Peter Nyers on "abject cosmopolitanism" (Nyers 2003). In the new preface of *The Location of Culture* for the "classic" edition, published by Routledge, Homi Bhabha contrasts his preferred "vernacular" to Julia Kristeva's "wounded" cosmopolitanism: "cosmopolitanism of the Trinidadian variety, figuratively speaking, that emerges from the world of migrant boarding-houses and the habitations of national and diasporic minorities. Julia Kristeva, in a different context, calls it a 'wounded cosmopolitanism.' In my view, it is better described as a vernacular cosmopolitanism which measures global progress from the minoritarian perspective. Its claims to freedom and equality are marked by a 'right to difference in equality'" (Bhabha 2004, pp. xvi–xvii; also see Bhabha 2001). The study of these and other qualified definitions of the cosmopolitan could be a subject of an entire research project.

8. For a more extended account of this "epic of En-lightenment," see Ossman 2002.

9. Indeed "From Kant and Herder through Dilthey and Nietzsche, generations of German writers contrasted conduct that is unthinking, habitual, and animal-like with conduct that is self conscious and willful" (Levine 2005, p. 108; also see Camic 1986). But one must ask whether habits are not only necessary but good. Might one work with and on one's habits in ways that include some kind

of considered willfulness? These questions will come up with respect to how serial migrants place themselves in positions that require the acquisition of habits without necessarily discarding old ones.

10. In this sense, the cosmopolitan subject might be related to what some commentators have seen as the "aesthetic" cosmopolitanism of late modernity. Motti Rgev writes: "In late modernity, however, the cultural uniqueness of nations and ethnic groups is no longer characterized by such a quest for exclusive, relatively isolated spaces of cultural content and aesthetic form. The quest for essentialist purism has been replaced by an admitted openness to late modern cultural forms. The orthodox commitment to a rigid form of nationalist culture has been replaced by a fluid conception of ethno-national uniqueness, one that is constantly and consciously willing to implement stylistic innovations in art and culture *from different parts of the world*" (Regev 2007; my italics). It is telling that Regev resorts to "different parts of the world."

11. Tazi 2007, p. 73.

12. On others, their particularity and variety, see Benhabib 1992; Appiah 2006. It is noteworthy that Benhabib (2006) also takes the issue of the "veil" as an object of debate in exploring cosmopolitanism.

13. I asked each of the people I interviewed for this research if they considered themselves to be cosmopolitans. Only two, who happened to be academics, said they were. The others associated cosmopolitanism with wealth, superficiality, or an obsession with material possessions and fashion.

14. Steele 1998, p. 75. On the Parisian also see "Paris n'existe pas," Rattier 1857.

15. Also see Cohen 2007 and the discussion of her sense of "service" in Chapter 5. I am not implying that the only borders are those between states; this is in fact one of the problems with how some of the cosmopolitan literature approaches difference, which leads to a way of understanding the world as a whole.

16. In some ways, Laurence might be seen as a precursor to the many young British citizens who increasingly "see themselves living elsewhere," according to an article in *Le Monde* (June 6, 2006), which cites Danny Srikansrajah, associate director of the Institute for Public Policy Research in the UK as saying that "the country should worry about seeing its children who are educated in its universities going to travel in other latitudes. The economy suffers from a lack of qualified labor. British youth are in the course of becoming one of the largest diasporas in the world" (my translation). One must also keep in mind that the teaching of English to non-native speakers is an extremely lucrative business.

17. See my account in Ossman 2007a.

18. What a difference from the youths of what has been called the "no-nation generation" described by Chrystia Freeland (yes, that is indeed her name!) in an upbeat opinion piece in the *Financial Times* as "cosmopolitan nomads": children of executives who grew up all over the world, people between fifteen and twenty-nine who say their national identities are fluid and that they "care" about the world as a whole (Freeland "The No Nation Generation," *Financial Times*: October 26 2007). Interestingly, she expresses the idea that it would be difficult to bring up children in several places: they would feel the pain of uprooting in a way that adults would not. But her interlocutors reassured her that this was not a problem, for with new information technologies one remains in touch, and besides, this was a good way to bring up a child "with a sense of global belonging—and global responsibility." Laurence's ideas are much more strategic; indeed, he reacts to the "global" claims as he has lived them out.

Also see the 2012 debate published in the *New York Times* regarding Americans migrating to get ahead: http://www.nytimes.com/roomfordebate/2012/01/08/is-the-us-still-a-land-of-opportunity/

19. See again Turner 2002 and Smith 2007.

20. On "Cosmopolitan Vision" see Beck 2006 and my reaction, Ossman 2006.

21. See, for instance, Hill 2000, Appiah 2006, and autobiographies cited as examples of cosmopolitanism, such as Said 2000 and Tuan 1999.

22. Discourses on immigration have become increasingly central to French and European political debate since the late 1980s. The rise of the National Front Party led by Jean-Marie Le Pen was indicative of this trend. The literature on this is extensive, and I will not pretend to summarize it here. As I have recounted elsewhere, this story is not foreign to my own becoming a serial migrant; the first article I published recounted the rise of the *S.O.S. Racisme* movement in France, an organization I knew from the inside (Ossman 1988). The rise of debates on immigration, then largely focused on "Arabs" from North Africa, led me to take an interest in the Maghreb, and then in 1988 to make my first attempts at multisite ethnography between Casablanca and Paris, in the context of the French presidential elections of that year in which Jean-Marie Le Pen received more than 14% of the vote (Ossman 1994).

23. Abouhouraira 2007, p. 162.

24. The literature on the Mediterranean as a culture zone, space of exchange, and actor of history is voluminous. Braudel's masterworks naturally come to

mind, but Leila's attention to daily practices and the land are perhaps more evocative of the work of anthropologists like Julio Caro-Baroja and Germaine Tillion, not to mention Pierre Bourdieu.

25. One thinks of Hamid Naficy's discussion of prospective nostalgia. See Naficy 2001.

CHAPTER 2

1. The nomad moves through smooth spaces, characterized by flows and continuity, whereas the state works to striate and settle migration. A political dialectic arises from this opposition of nomadic motion to the settling powers of the state.

2. We might question the nomad's ability to converse; is this a sense of powerlessness or an affirmation of his intrinsic lack of questioning of his own power to progress? Might being unwilling to engage in dialogue be a sign of power that need not seek legitimation?

3. For more on mobility and speed, see, for instance, Cresswell 2006; but also note his manner of framing his work with the "Western World." This may be taken as a sign of modesty, but the problem of knowing where this "world" is and when one is in its presence is not at all straightforward; how might one frame the processes he discusses in terms of an opposition of the West to the rest? This is in itself problematic. It recalls the way that some seek equality for all through inclusion in cosmopolitanism through hyphenation.

4. The term is used by geologists to talk about the layering process of sedimentation. In medicine, striated muscle is contrasted to smooth muscle.

5. Casey 1997, p. 307.

6. The notion of "giving off" impressions is of course a nod to Erving Goffman (Goffman 1959).

7. Deleuze and Guattari 2003, p. 287.

8. One aspect of this consolidation has to do with creating an image of the subject or the nation. See, for instance, Mattern 2008.

9. Mai 2007.

10. Mai also writes extensively about the inability of those who engage in casual homosexual relationships to acknowledge themselves as gay (Mai 2009).

11. Goldschmidt 2006.

12. Collyer 2010; also see Agier 2011, Doná and Voutira 2007. The different legislations and practices concerning migration have been a point of contention among the states that signed the Schengen Agreement in 1985, and since the

convention to implement it in 1990. Europe of course has no territory of its own. For more on European migration policy, see Nascimbene 2008.

13. One might compare Benedict Anderson's classic account of the forms of altruistic behavior attributable to the national imagination (Anderson 1983). In this case, the actions taken are not in the name of some imagined group; these men know one another, some superficially, others because they have traveled together for weeks or months. Yet it is not camaraderie but the sense of a common project, a common goal, that leads them to make the kinds of altruistic sacrifice Anderson wonders at with respect to national sentiment. One must wonder whether they do not feel some sense of vindication against the powers that would contain the free movement of people simply because they were born in a particular location each time someone makes it over the fence and to the office where one might ask for asylum.

14. These scenes date from 2005; see Laacher 2007, especially p. 147. Only a few months later, most of the would-be migrants were returned to their countries of origin after the Moroccan army stormed their camps. A few stragglers stayed on in Morocco (http://www.rfi.fr/actufr/articles/077/article_43405.asp). For a personal account of trans-Saharan migration, see, for instance, Lépine's presentation of the account he recorded in Morocco of Jean Paul Dzokou-Newo's migration (Lépine 2006).

15. See Derrida's and Habermas's conversations with Giovanna Borradori (Borradori 2003).

16. The romance with mobility is not independent of the spatial turn; more on this later.

17. I had the pleasure of staying in a lovely apartment above *al riwaq* gallery while in Manama. I thank everyone there for their hospitality and for their moving reactions to the paper I presented there in relation to projections of my paintings about war, later published in Ossman 2010.

18. On February 22, 2011, one hundred thousand people demonstrated in Bahrain, out of a total population of five hundred thousand (Michael Slackman and Nadim Audi, "Protests in Bahrain Become Test of Wills," *New York Times*, Feb. 22, 2011).

19. Madawi Rachid points out the scope of the much larger "kingdom without borders" (Rachid, 2009).

20. As in the case of many of the other uprisings of the Arab Spring of 2011, few reports indicated that many of these were made possible by a long history of protests, not just by Facebook.

21. Thus countering Marc Auge's idea of *non-lieux*, non-places (Auge 1995).

22. See Hertzfeld 1992.

23. One might consider how states achieve a greater or lesser degree of conformity to such definitions.

24. The problem is not simply one of what Ong (2000) has called a "gradation of sovereignty." It is not a matter of scale but of kind, a question of recognizing how different worlds that define the person, the citizen, or even the human are not only profoundly different, but become ever more necessary to identify as the coordination of movements of many kinds becomes an increasingly vital aspect of all kinds of power.

25. Thus, new projects for bringing in guestworkers are taking form in Europe and the United States. See Papademetiou et al. 2009; Agunias 2008; Venurini 2008; Vervotec 2007.

26. The interpenetration of routes of migration and fabrication, not just commerce, are changing; see Rachel Donadio, "Chinese Remake the 'Made in Italy' Fashion Label," *New York Times*, Sept. 13, 2011. Also see Goldin et al. 2011; Papademetriou et al. 2009.

27. Madawi Rachid points out that much of the research carried out in the region has been on migration but notes also the extent to which "locals" are wary of being "creolized" or rendered "inauthentic" due to the influx of foreigners (Rachid 2005, p. 3). Some maintain the idea that this mass influx of immigrants is only temporary, but this seems unlikely. My objective is not to offer an in-depth exploration of these topics or an outlook regarding the settlement or departure of these populations, but for more, see Rachid 2005, and also Gardner and Nagy 2008.

28. For a fascinating firsthand account and analysis of the pilgrimage by the anthropologist Abdellah Hammoudi, see Hammoudi 2006.

29. See Ossman 1994.

30. See Rachid 1991 for an account of the early tribal rivalries that made the kingdom what it is today.

31. As Ahmed Kanna notes, the complexity of the relationship with Iran is nothing new. He writes: "Indeed, the majority of Dubai citizens today are ethnically Iranian. Although the Dubai rulers, enabled by oil wealth and imperial protection, have largely co-opted or otherwise marginalized nationalist and reformist aspirations, they remain sensitive to representations of their Arab authenticity or lack thereof" (Kanna 2010, p. 104). There is also a large contingent of Iranian traders and immigrants among those who circulate in the region. See, for instance, Adelkhah 2005.

32. Yes, his resources are impressive when compared to those of most of the people from the subcontinent one meets in Manama, yet this rootless man has made it clear that the stability of his marriage depends on his providing the standard of living that his wife is accustomed to.

33. Verlan, the slang of the French suburbs, involves inversion of syllables. See, for instance, Silverstein 2004; Jerad 2007.

34. See Ossman and Terrio 2006.

35. See Derrida, 2000 and Borradori 2003.

CHAPTER 3

1. Sayad 1999.

2. Nancy Green has noted the influence of the story of migration to America on the models used to study migration (Green 2002).

3. This explains, for instance, the rise of immigration as a major object of political discourse in Western Europe once it became apparent that the guest workers brought in as laborers began staying and bringing their families. Debates about "circular migration" are again bringing to the fore discussions about guest worker programs and the implications of settlement and return migration. For a critical approach to such policy discussions, see Vertovec 2007. For the ways these may shift the way "settler" nations weave immigration into their collective histories, see Pellerin 2011. For an outline of approaches to circular migration at the intersection of anthropology and geography, see Gidwani and Sivaramakrishnan 2003.

4. Indeed, as Ian Goldin, Geoffrey Cameron, and Meera Balajaran note, "Migration is not a problem to be solved; it is an intrinsic element of international society and inextricably bound up with globalization itself" (Goldin, Cameron, and Balajaran 2011, p. 260). The nature of this interweaving, however, needs to be further elucidated; it is not enough to establish typologies of those whose migration is considered forced or desired, or accounts of how free circulation would benefit the world economy. These authors aim to influence policy, but it seems that what is needed even for this is a leap of the imagination regarding how different process of migration make people into subjects that are not reducible to function or ethnicity.

5. Bhabha, drawing on Gasché's interpretation of Walter Benjamin and on Benjamin himself, writes: "I am more engaged with the 'foreign' element that reveals the interstitial; insists in the textile superfluity of folds and wrinkles; and becomes the 'unstable element of linkage,' the indeterminate temporality of the in-between, that has to be engaged in creating the conditions through which

'newness comes into the world.' The foreign element 'destroys the original's structures of reference and sense communication as well' not simply by negating it but by negotiating the disjunction in which successive cultural temporalities are 'preserved in the work of history and at the same time cancelled" (Bhabha 1994, pp. 227–28). One cannot help but associate such ideas not only with Benjamin but with Deleuze, both because of the metaphorical suggestiveness of this link and because of how the "foreign element" creates newness through destruction in ways reminiscent of the nomad. Yet while the body of Deleuze and Guattari's nomad is also his mode of locomotion and his dwelling and while the region he roams is expansive, Bhabha's alien is simply an "element of linkage." But the source of the alien's energy is unclear. Might it simply be derived from the motion of the edges of worlds between which he is situated? If this is the case, then what he is describing is simply a kind of inversion of the "clash of cultures." For another interpretation of this passage from Bhabha, see Ossman 2002, pp. 156–57.

6. See, for instance, Ahmed et al. 2003; Brettell 2003; Kaplan 1996; Levitt 2001, 2009; Ong 1999, 2006.

7. As I noted in the previous chapter, a bridge connects the Eastern province of Saudi Arabia to the island of Bahrain. Bahrain is considered an "easier" place to live than Saudi Arabia for those who come from elsewhere, because there are fewer constraints on practices like drinking and fewer obligations such as prayer.

8. See, for instance, Calhoun 2002 on business travelers, as well as the essays assembled in Amit 2007.

9. The bibliography regarding efforts to develop a typology of various kinds of people on the move could be very long indeed. Clifford 1997 and Hannerz 1991 had a formative influence on the debates that have since led to ever more finely tuned efforts to break down various categories into more precise definitions of specific kinds of travelers. Arjun Appadurai and John Urry have suggested more integrated approaches to migration as part of wider patterns of circulation and mobility (Appadurai 1996; Urry 2000, 2007).

10. I met Bashir in 2005; since that time Dubai has experienced the effects of the worldwide economic crisis in a typically spectacular fashion. See, for instance, Joshua Hammer, "Good-bye to Dubai," *New York Review of Books*, Aug. 19, 2010 (http://www.nybooks.com/articles/archives/2010/aug/19/good-bye-dubai/).

11. Very few of the dozens of people I met in the course of this study could afford to maintain more than one place of residence.

12. For more on the journalists who work in these newsrooms, see Mellor 2011.

13. See for instance, Goldin, Cameron, and Balajaran 2011, pp. 168–69.

14. See Ossman 2007b, pp. 201–18.

15. Indeed, it was the idea of a common ground, not a common story, that oriented my initial foray into the study of serial migration. See Ossman 2007b.

16. White 1999, p. 8.

17. He writes: "For competing narratives are differences among the modes of emplotments which predominate in them. It is because narratives are always emplotted that they are meaningfully comparable: it is because narratives are differently emplotted that discriminations among the types of plot can be made" (White 1999, p. 30).

18. I am not suggesting that other forms of recollections do not intervene, but I do see a structured setting of interval against interval in the way that people recount the "internal conversations" (Archer 2003) that they have at the moment of departure. Thus, I cannot interpret this situation in terms of the utter free-flow quality that Turner associates with liminality. It is important to note that he limits his subjects' imagination by reference to a cultural context, which might lead to a lack of attention to the importance of such "abstract" or structured sequences (he saw this kind of approach as tainted by "Gallic structuralism").

19. But as Michael Oakeshott notes in his essay on history, the units in a series will change one another; each unit in the series "comments" on the other terms, and the addition of new members in the set leads to a change in the meaning of each of the other members. He writes: "But judgment involves more than a series, it involves a world. And the view that history is concerned with what is merely successive breaks down. What was taken for a mere series has turned, on our hands, into a world. For, whatever the terms of a 'series' so far lose their isolation and come to depend upon the criticism and guarantee of other, perhaps subsequent, terms, and of the 'series' as a whole, there is no longer a mere series of what is successive, but a world of what is co-existent" (Oakeshott 1995 [orig. 1933], p. 91). He notes that this worldmaking creates an experience—and "the process of all experience is to make a given world more of a world, to make it coherent" (p. 96). The extent to which a serial migrant can create a "world" is something we need to be skeptical about. Yet it is worth considering how some move from place to place as a way of making a life more of a life. More on this in the following chapter.

20. Van Gennep 1960.

21. Victor Turner suggests that rituals become less important in "advanced societies" in which the liminal comes to be found in play. See Turner 1982, pp. 27–29.

22. See Ossman 2007a, introduction.

23. Turner 1974, p. 255.

24. Ibid., p. 133.

25. Pierre Bourdieu, *Pascalian Meditations*, cited in Hoy 2009, p. 213. See also Bourdieu 1977 on practice.

CHAPTER 4

1. Francastel 1970, pp. 112–13 (my translation).

2. The secular examples of these works might also be analyzed for what they imply about a shared social order: for now, I focus on the more explicit narrative element that is most apparent in the Christ story.

3. Thus, Nelson Goodman notes that "A true version is true in some worlds, a false version in none. Thus, the multiple worlds of conflicting true versions are actual worlds, not the merely possible worlds or nonworlds of false versions." He continues: "So if there is any actual world, there are many. For there are conflicting true versions and they cannot be true in the same world. If the notion of a multiplicity of actual worlds is odd and unpalatable, we nevertheless seem forced to it by the intolerable alternative of a world in which contradictory and therefore all versions are true" (Goodman 1984, p. 31).

4. Benhabib 2005, pp. 673–77.

5. I would need several volumes to adequately explore how tropes of assemblage and *bricolage*, not to mention hybridity, have been deployed in academic discussions. See, for instance, Morley 2000, pp. 232–33, for a discussion of "hybridity talk." Rather than surveying the vast literature, I narrow my focus here to suggest that the serial migrant demonstrates some of the ways in which these notions avoid the real issues. The serial migrant is a complex subject not simply because it can include several individuals, but because it involves a confrontation within itself of various ways of making up the world and framing it. As James Faubion notes, individual human beings are capable of autopoiesis only "after a considerable course of socialization has taken place, only after a considerable dose of the intersubjective has already been incorporated, already become part of the self (and hence are never individuals in their pure individuality). Without such a supplement, they—we—would be little more than what Clifford Geertz aptly termed some time ago 'basket cases'" (Faubion 2011, pp. 119–20). Serial migrants often speak about their situation as one of "being too much," but at the same time they valorize the way they can "take it, take it in and make it my own," as Hader put it. If indeed we were a collection of each possible self from each of

the systems that made us, we would, as Faubion says, be basket cases, but serial migrants would be even more so, because the accumulation of social identities, statuses, positions, and habits is not simply messy but, taken all at once, terrifying. By working through borders serial migrants seek to control accumulation without relinquishing the specificity of their experience. Their essentializing references to systems of state, society, or culture enable them to an often ironic pointing to the inability of any state to hold them to a system of making sense of themselves.

6. See Hoy 2009, p. xvii.

7. Foucault 1988, p. 84. The original reads:

Alors que l'éthique ancien impliquait une articulation très serre du pouvoir sur soi et du pouvoir sur les autres, et devait donc se référer a une esthétique de la vie en conformité avec le statut, les règles nouvelles du jeu politique rendent plus difficile la définition des rapports entre ce qu'on est, ce qu'on peut faire et ce qu'on est tenu d'accomplir: la constitution de soi-même comme sujet éthique de ses propres actions devient plus problématique. (Foucault 1984b, p. 105).

8. Foucault 1984b, p. 106.

9. In fact, although Romanians and Bulgarians can now travel and reside in other EU nations, they do not have the same immigration rights as other EU citizens. Employers and migrants remain confused about their status. Hugo Brady notes: "The majority now have no restrictions on workers from those countries that joined the EU in 2004. But a large number have maintained restrictions on Bulgaria and Romania. The exceptions are Cyprus, the Czech Republic, Estonia, Finland, Latvia, Lithuania, Poland, Slovakia, Slovenia and Sweden. From 2014, the period of transition will end and there will be complete free movement of workers between all member-states. However, EU countries can still close labour markets in an emergency, if the Commission approves the decision" (European Centre for Reform, *Briefing, EU Migration Policy A-Z*, 2008, p. 13).

10. For a sobering glimpse into how Romanian minors and other "immigrants"—many of whom were born in France—are perceived by the French juvenile justice system, see Terrio 2009; also see Mai 2007.

11. Kenbib 1999.

12. Cohen 2007, p. 92.

13. Agamben 2007, p. 99.

14. Hoy 2009, p. 59.

15. Oakeshott 1995, p. 91.

16. This contrasts with Ong's "flexible citizens" (Ong 1999). Perhaps, as

she suggests, there is a "cultural logic" at work in the Chinese family networks she examines, yet it may also be the case that if one defines the object of study according to ethnicity, one comes up with conclusions that tend to support the idea of a cultural logic as fundamental.

17. Francastel 1970, pp. 112–13.

18. For more on the subject of maids, see, for instance, Brody 2006, Leonard 2003, Nagy 1998, and Ong 2006.

19. Also see Leila Abouhouraira's account of Assad's story in Abouhouraira 2007, pp. 166–67.

20. There are no Moroccan Christians except a few converts who have been intermittently subjected to trial; conversion from Islam to other religions is not permitted by law.

21. For more on the use of American names in Casablanca, see Ossman 1994.

22. Oakeshott 1995, pp. 91.

CHAPTER 5

1. See Ossman 2010 and the other essays in the same volume.

2. Marilyn Strathern offers an elegant reading of questions of figuration and background in her analysis of four photographs with the people taken out. In viewing these images, she writes, "What you see instead of a world filled with other persons is a world in which this or that human, individual, interpreter offers his or her particular and singular perspective. That perspective can always be dwarfed by phenomena of a quite different order" (Strathern 2002, p. 109). She thus signals the pitfalls of a certain concept of the individual as appearing against the ground that she says is "perhaps the result of American conceptions of time and space." This tendency seems most marked in the social sciences: one might recall Simmel with his notion of the "individualistic" person as being outside of any system. One might also wonder whether the medium might be at issue; is not the photograph a promise of a certain notion of reality? I will suggest some similar ideas in the next chapter with respect to the "missing persons" in Bachelard's phenomenological approach to the space.

3. Bachelard 1981, p. 26.

4. On drawing and ethnographic field notes, see Hendrickson 2008 and Taussig 2011.

5. Cohen 2007, p. 92.

6. Ibid.

7. White 1999, p. 88.

8. This suspicion was perhaps most apparent in the days after 9/11. See Ossman 2007, introduction.

9. Archer 2007, p. 86.

10. Thus, in contrast to authors like Anthony Giddens or Ulrich Beck, I see this discourse of "En-lightenment" as central to modern life but note how it often obscures relevant social differences and strategies (Ossman 2002).

11. John Urry's call for a more "mobile" sociology or a "sociology without societies" (Urry 2000, 2007) can be cited here. I sense a common impulse in his writing and the ideas I am trying to work out through the study of serial migration. Mine, however, is certainly a more modest and more concrete proposal, given that it is less concerned with movement and more with the problems posed by settlement. For another take on governmentality and the "death of the social," also see Miller and Rose 2008, pp. 84–113.

12. Archer 2007, p. 257.

13. Ibid., pp. 69–70.

14. For more on the problems of context, location, and ethnography, see Gupta and Ferguson 1997, Gingrich and Fox 2002, Melhuus 2002, and Rabinow et al. 2008.

15. This was in the 1990s, before the revision of the *moudawana* or personal code.

16. The practice of passport accumulation would be an interesting topic of further study in itself; for more on citizenship and flexibility, see Ong's now-classic work on this topic (Ong 1999).

17. Foucault notes that the care of the self is always a taking into account of others, a matter of working toward a relationship with others that, while not denying the fact that power is always present in relations, might minimize domination. Majid's idea of the good life is not in amassing precious objects as a sign of his special status or in receiving special services as a tribute to one's economic power or social standing. Instead, his sense of the good emerges from a liberty of observing the relative deprivation of others. A reasoned, considered, exercised freedom to move toward a social world in which some collective good might be realized by a valuing of collective "comfort" that often includes a form of self-dispossession. See Foucault 2001, pp. 1533, 1546.

18. I have used this model of three worlds to interpret the politics of the wedding of the king of Morocco and to examine the publicity surrounding the wives of political leaders in the Arab world in Ossman 2007c and Ossman 2011, respectively.

19. For more on gossip, proximity and politics see Ossman 2007c and 2011.

20. Also see Strathern 2002.

21. On fixation, see Bachelard 1981, p. 25.

CHAPTER 6

1. Bachelard 1994, p. 61 (pp. 68–69 in 1981 edition in French).

2. Ibid., p. 56, then p. 61.

3. Bachelard recognizes that his emphasis on "intimacy" differs from the study of the "path." The house appears in a dynamic relation to this path. Ibid., pp. 10–12.

4. Casey 1997.

5. Ibid.

6. Instrumental assumptions regarding immigrants' motivations and practices surface again. Issues of marriage for papers are widely present in popular discussions about immigration, and sex is certainly one of the hottest topics on the immigration reading lists of graduate students these days, but despite that, love, affection, and the variety of emotions that bind people and lead them to embrace a place are either taken for granted or set aside in most research on the subject of migration. For more see Riaño and Baghdadi 2007.

7. On the history of the notion of communication, see Peters 1999.

8. Early 2007. Anthropologists call it "marrying the field" when they enter a relationship with someone from a research site.

REFERENCES

Abouhouraira, Leila. 2007. "In Search of Tangiers Past." In *The Places We Share: Migration, Subjectivity and Global Mobility,* ed. S. Ossman. Lanham, MD: Lexington Press.

Adelkhah, Fariba. 2005. "Les migrants prodigues. Pratiques notabiliaires des migrants iraniens dans le Golfe." In *Mondes en mouvements: Migrants et migrations au Moyen-Orient au tournant du XXIème siècle*, ed. Hana Jaber and France Métral. Beyrouth: IFPO.

Agamben, Giorgio. 2007. *Infancy and History: The Destruction of Experience*, trans. Liz Heron. London: Verso.

———. 1999. *Potentialities: Collected Essays in Philosophy*. Ed. and trans. Daniel Heller-Roazen. Stanford: Stanford University Press.

Agier, Michel. 2011. *Managing the Undesirables: Refugee Camps and Humanitarian Government*. London: Polity Press.

Ahmed, S., C. Casteneda, A. Fortier, and M. Sheller. 2003. *Uprootings/Regroundings: Questions of Home and Migration*. Oxford and New York: Berg.

Amit, Vered. 2007. *Going First Class? New Approaches to Privileged Travel and Movement*. New York: Berghan Books.

Anderson, Benedict. 1983. *Imagined Communities: Reflections on the Origins and Spread of Nationalism*. London: Verso.

———. 1998. "Nationalism, Identity and the World in Motion: On the Logics of Seriality." In *Cosmopolitics: Thinking and Feeling Beyond the Nation*, ed. P. Cheah and B. Robbins. Minneapolis: University of Minnesota Press.

Appadurai, Arjun. 1996. *Modernity at Large: Cultural Dimensions of Globalization*. Minneapolis: University of Minnesota Press.

Appiah, Anthony. 2006. *Cosmopolitanism: Ethics in a World of Strangers*. New York: W. W. Norton.

Archer, Margaret. 2003. *Structure, Agency and the Internal Conversation*. Cambridge: Cambridge University Press.

———. 2007. *Making Our Way through the World*. Cambridge: Cambridge University Press.

Archibugi, Daniele, ed. 2003. *Debating Cosmopolitics*. London: Verso.

Augé, Marc. 1995. *Non-Places: Introduction to an Anthropology of Supermodernity*, trans. John Howe. London: Verso.

Bachelard, Gaston. 1994. *The Poetics of Space*, trans. Maria Jolas. Boston: Beacon. (1981. *La Poétique de l'Espace*. 10th ed. [first pub. 1957]. Paris: Presses Universitaires de France.)

Bataglia, Deborah, ed. 1995. *Rhetorics of Self-Making*. Berkeley: University of California Press.

Beck, Ulrich. 2001. "The Cosmopolitan Society and Its Enemies." *Politologiske Studier* 4 (no. 2, May).

———. 2006. *Cosmopolitan Vision*, trans. Ciaran Cronin. London: Polity.

Beck, Ulrich, and Nathan Sznaider. 2010. "Unpacking Cosmopolitanism for the Social Sciences: A Research Agenda." *British Journal of Sociology* 57 (no. 1, Jan.): 381–403.

Benhabib, Seyla. 1992. *Situating the Self: Gender, Community, and Postmodernism in Contemporary Ethics*. New York: Routledge.

———. 2005. "Borders, Boundaries and Citizenship." *Political Science and Politics* 38: 673–77.

———. 2006. *Another Cosmopolitanism*. Oxford and New York: Oxford University Press.

Bhabha, Homi. 2004. *The Location of Culture*, 2nd ed. (first pub. 1994). London: Routledge.

———. 2001. "UnSatisfied: Notes on Vernacular Cosmopolitanism." In *Postcolonial Discourses*, ed. Gregory Castle. pp. 38–52. London: Blackwell.

Borradori, Giovanna. 2003. *Philosophy in a Time of Terror: Dialogues with Jurgen Habermas and Jacques Derrida*. Chicago: University of Chicago Press.

Bourdieu, Pierre. 1977. *Outline of a Theory of Practice*. Translated by Richard Nice. Cambridge: Cambridge University Press.

———. 1980. *Le Sens Pratique*. Paris: Les Éditions de minuit.

Braudel, Fernand. 1982. *La Méditerranée et le Monde Méditerranéen à l'Epoque de Philippe II*. Paris: Armand Colin.

Breckenridge, C. A., S. Pollock, H. K. Bhabha, and D. Chakrabarty. 2002. *Cosmopolitanism*. Durham: Duke University Press.

Bretell, Caroline B. 2003. *Anthropology and Migration: Essays on Transnationalism, Ethnicity, and Identity*. Walnut Creek, CA: Altamira Press.

———. 2007. "Adjustment of Status, Remittances, and Return: Some Observations on 21st Century Migration Processes." *City and Society* 19 (no. 1, June): 47–59.

Brody, Alyson. 2006. "Indian Nurses in the Gulf from Job Opportunity to Life Strategy." In *Migrant Women and Work*, ed. A. Agrawal. London and Thousand Oaks, CA: Sage.

Brubaker, Rogers. 2006. *Ethnicity without Groups*. Cambridge: Harvard University Press.

Calhoun, Craig. 2003. "Belonging in the Cosmopolitan Imaginary." *Ethnicities* 3 (no. 4): 531–68.

Camic, Charles. 1986. "The Matter of Habit." *American Journal of Sociology* 91 (no. 5, March): 1039–87.

Casey, Edward S. 1997. *The Fate of Place*. Berkeley: University of California Press.

Cassarino, Jean-Pierre. 2004. "Theorising Return Migration: The Conceptual Approach to Return Migrants Revisited." *International Journal on Multicultural Societies* 6 (no. 2): 253–79.

Certeau, Michel de. 1984. *The Practice of Everyday Life*. Berkeley: University of California Press.

Cheah, Phen, and Bruce Robbins, eds. 1998. *Cosmopolitics: Thinking and Feeling Beyond the Nation*. Minneapolis: University of Minnesota Press.

Clifford, James. 1997. *Routes, Travel and Translation in the Late Twentieth Century*. Cambridge: Harvard University Press.

Cohen, Shana. 2007. "A New Take on the Wandering Jew." In *The Places We Share: Migration, Subjectivity and Global Mobility*, ed. S. Ossman. Lanham, MD: Lexington Press.

Coleman, Simon, and Peter Collins, eds. 2006. *Locating the Field: Space, Place and Context in Anthropology*. Oxford: Berg.

Collyer, Michael. 2010. "Stranded Migrants and the Fragmented Journey." *Journal of Refugee Studies* 23 (no. 3): 273–93.

Creswell, Tim. 2006. *On the Move: Mobility in the Modern Western World*. New York: Routledge.

Dayan-Herzbrun, Sonia, and Etienne Tassun, eds. 2005. "Citoyennetés Cosmo-politiques." *Tumultes* 24 (May).

Deleuze, Gilles, and Félix Guattari. 1968. *Différence et Répétition*. Paris: Presses Universitaires de France.

———. 1980. *Capitalisme et Schizophrénie 2: Mille Plateaux*. Paris: Les Éditions de Minuit.

———. 2003. "From 1227: Treatise on Nomadology; The War Machine." In *Modernism to Postmodernism: An Anthology*, ed. L. E. Cahoone. London: Blackwell.

Derrida, Jacques. 2000. *Of Hospitality*, trans. Anne Dufourmantelle. Stanford: Stanford University Press.

Doná, Giorgia, with E. Voutira. 2007. "Refugee Research Methodologies: Consolidation and Transformation of a Field." *Journal of Refugee Studies* 20 (no. 2): 163–71.

Elden, Stuart. 2001. *Mapping the Present, Heiddeger, Foucault and the Project of a Spatial History*. London: Continuum.

Faubion, James D. 2001. *The Shadows and Lights of Waco: Millenialism Today*. Princeton: Princeton University Press.

———. 2011. *The Anthropology of Ethics*. Cambridge: Cambridge University Press.

Foucault, Michel. 1984a. *Histoire de la sexualité*, vol. 2, *L'usage des plaisirs*. Paris: Gallimard.

———. 1984b. *Histoire de la sexualité*, vol. 3, *Le souci de soi*. Paris: Gallimard. (English translation Foucault 1988.)

———. 1988. *The History of Sexuality*, vol. 3: *The Care of the Self*, trans. Robert Hurely. New York: Vintage.

———. 2001. "L'éthique du souci de soi comme pratique de la liberté." In *Dits et écrits II, 1976–1988*, pp. 1527–48. Paris: Gallimard/le Seuil.

———. 2009. "Le courage de la Vérité; le gouvernement de soi et des autres." *Cours au collège de France, 1984*. Paris: Gallimard/le Seuil.

Francastel, Pierre. 1970. *Etudes de sociologie de l'art, création picturale et société*. Paris: Denoël.

———. 1983. *L'Image, la Vision et l'Imagination, de la Peinture au Cinéma*. Paris: Denoël/Gonthier.

Freeland, Chrystia. 2007. "The No Nation Generation." *Financial Times*, 26 October.

Frisby, David, and Mike Featherstone, eds. 1987. *Simmel on Culture: Selected Writings*. London: Sage.

Gardner, Andrew, and Sharon Nagy, eds. 2008. "Introduction, New Ethnographic Fieldwork among Migrants, Residents and Citizens in the Arab States of the Gulf," *City and Society* 20 (no. 1): 1–4.

Gidwany, Vinary, and K. Sivaramakrishnan. 2003. "Circular Migration and the Spaces of Cultural Assertion." *Annals of the Association of American Geographers* 93 (no. 1): 186–213.

Gingrich, Andre, and Richard G. Fox, eds. 2002. *Anthropology by Comparison*. London: Routledge.

Goffman, Erving. 1959. *The Presentation of Self in Everyday Life*. New York: Anchor Books.

Goldin, Ian, Geoffrey Cameron, and Meera Balajaran. 2011. *Exceptional People. How Migration Shaped Our World and Will Define Our Future*. Princeton: Princeton University Press.

Goodman, Nelson. 1978. *Ways of Worldmaking*. Indianapolis: Hackett.

———. 1984. *Of Mind and Other Matters*. Cambridge, MA: Harvard University Press.

Green, Nancy. 2002. *Penser les migrations*. Paris: Presses Universitaires de France.

Gupta, A., and J. Ferguson. 1997. *Anthropological Locations: Boundaries and Grounds of a Field Science*. Berkeley: University of California Press.

Habermas, Jurgen. 1984. *Reason and the Rationalization of Society*, vol. 1 of *The Theory of Communicative Action*, trans. Thomas McCarthy. Boston: Beacon Press.

Hammoudi, Abdellah. 2006. *A Season in Mecca: Narrative of a Pilgrimage*. New York: Hill and Wang.

Hannerz, Ulf. 1996. "Cosmopolitans and Locals in World Culture." In *Transnational Connections: Culture, People, Places*, ed. U. Hannerz. New York: Routledge.

Harvey, David. 2001. *Spaces of Capital: Towards a Critical Geography*. New York: Routledge.

Hendrickson, Carol. 2008. "Visual Field Notes: Drawing Insights in the Yucatan." *Visual Anthropology Review*, 24 (no. 2): 117–32.

Heidegger, Martin. 1962. *Being and Time*, trans. John Macquarrie and Edward Robinson. New York: Harper and Row.

———. 1971. "Building Dwelling Thinking." In *Poetry, Language, Thought*, trans. Albert Hofstadter. New York: Harper and Row.

Herzfeld, Michael. 1992. *The Social Production of Indifference: Exploring the Symbolic Roots of Western Bureaucracy*. Chicago: University of Chicago Press.

Hill, Jason D. 2000. *Becoming a Cosmopolitan: What It Means to Be Human in the New Millennium*. Lanham, MD: Rowman and Littlefield.

Hoy, David C. 2009. *The Time of Our Lives: A Critical History of Temporality*. Cambridge, MA: MIT Press.

Ibn Khaldun, 2004. *The Muqaddimah: An Introduction to History*, trans. Franz Rosenthal. Princeton: Princeton University Press.

Jerad, Nabiha. 2007. "From the Maghreb to the Mediterranean. Immigration and Transnational Locations." In *The Places We Share: Migration, Subjectivity and Global Mobility*, ed. S. Ossman. Lanham, MD: Lexington Press.

Kanna, Ahmed. 2010. "Flexible Citizenship in Dubai: Neoliberal Subjectivity in the Emerging 'City-Corporation.'" *Cultural Anthropology* 25 (no. 1): 100–129.

Kaplan, Caren. 1996. *Questions of Travel: Postmodern Discourses of Displacement*. Durham, NC: Duke University Press.

Kenbib, Mohammed. 1999. "Les migrations des juifs marocains à l'époque contemporaine." In *Migrations internationales entre le Maghreb et l'Europe*, ed. M. Berriane and H. Popp. Rabat: Université Mohammed V.

Kristeva, Julia. 1994. *Strangers to Ourselves*, trans. Leon S. Roudiez. New York: Columbia University Press.

Laacher, Smain. 2007. *Le peuple des clandestins*. Paris: Calmann-Levy.

Lamont, Michèle, and Sada Aksartova. 2002. "Ordinary Cosmopolitanisms: Strategies for Bridging Racial Boundaries among Working-Class Men." *Theory, Culture and Society* 19 (no. 4): 1–25.

Latour, Bruno. 2005. *Reassembling the Social: An Introduction to Actor-Network Theory*. Oxford: Oxford University Press.

Lefebvre, Henri. 1991. *The Production of Space*, trans. Donald Nicholson Smith. London: Blackwell.

Leonard, Karen. 2003. "South Asian Women in the Gulf: Families and Futures Reconfigured." *Trans-Status Subjects: Gender in the Globalization of South and Southeast Asia*, ed. S. Earker and E. Esha Niyogi. Durham, NC: Duke University Press.

Lépine, Joseph. 2006. *Une Marche en Liberté—émigration subsaharienne— présentation de Jean-Paul Dzokou-Newo: la traverse d'un enfer européen au Maghreb*. Paris: Maisonneuve et Larose.

Levin, David Michael, ed. 1993. *Modernity and the Hegemony of Vision*. Berkeley: University of California Press.

Levine, Donald N. 2005. "The Continuing Challenge of Weber's Theory of Rational Action." In *Max Weber's Economy and Society: A Critical Companion*, ed. C. Camic, P. Gorski, and D. Trubeck. Palo Alto: Stanford University Press.

Levitt, Peggy. 2001. *The Transnational Villagers*. Berkeley: University of California Press.

———. 2004. "Redefining the Boundaries of Belonging: The Institutional Character of Transnational Religious Life." *Sociology of Religion* 65 (no. 1): 1–18.

———. 2009. "Routes and Routes: Understanding the Lives of the Second Generation Transnationally." *Journal of Ethnic and Racial Studies* 35 (no. 7): 1225–42.

Maalki, Liisa. 1992. "National Geographic: The Rooting of Peoples and the Territorialization of National Identity among Scholars and Refugees." *Cultural Anthropology* 7 (no. 1): 24–44.

Malinowski, Bronislaw. 1961. *Argonauts of the Western Pacific*. New York: E. P. Dutton.

Mai, Nicola. 2007. "'Errance,' Migration and Male Sex Work: On the Socio-Cultural Sustainability of a Third Space." In *The Places We Share: Migration, Subjectivity and Global Mobility*, ed. S. Ossman. Lanham, MD: Lexington Press.

———. 2009. "Between Minor and Errant Mobility: The Relation between the Psychological Dynamics and the Migration Patterns of Young Men Selling Sex in the EU." *Mobilities* 4 (no. 3): 349–66.

Malpas, Jeff. 1999. *Place and Experience: A Philosophical Topology*. Cambridge: Cambridge University Press.

———. 2006. *Heidegger's Topology*. Cambridge, MA: MIT Press.

Marcus, George. 1995. "On Eccentricity." In *Rhetorics of Self-Making*, ed. D. Bataglia. Berkeley: University of California Press.

———. 1998. *Ethnography through Thick and Thin*. Princeton: Princeton University Press.

———. 2007. "Collaborative Imaginaries." *Taiwan Journal of Anthropology* 5 (no. 1): 1–17.

———. 2011. "Affinities: Fieldwork in Anthropology Today and the Ethnographic in Artwork." In *Art and Anthropology*, ed. A. Schneider and C. Wright. Oxford: Berg.

Massey, Doreen B. 2005. *For Space*. London and Thousand Oaks, CA: Sage.

Mattern, Sharon. 2008. "Font of a Nation: Creating a National Graphic Identity for Qatar." *Public Culture* 20 (no. 3): 479–96.

Melhuus, Merit. 2002. "Issues of Relevance: Anthropology and the Challenges of Cross-Cultural Comparison." In *Anthropology by Comparison*, ed. A. Gingrich and R. Fax. London: Routledge.

Mellor, Noha. 2011. *Arab Journalists in Transnational Media*. New York: Hampton Press.

Miller, Peter, and Nicolas S. Rose. 2008. *Governing the Present: Administering Economic, Social and Personal Life*. London: Polity.

Mirkin, Barry. 2010. *Population Levels, Trends and Policies in the Arab Region: Challenges and Opportunities*. United National Development Program, Regional Bureau for Arab States.

Morley, David. 2000. *Home Territories: Media, Mobility, and Identity*. London and New York: Routledge.

Mulhall, Stephen. 1991. *On Being in the World: Wittgenstein and Heidegger and Seeing Aspects*. London: Routledge.

Naficy, Hamid. 2001. *An Accented Cinema: Exilic and Diasporic Filmmaking*. Princeton: Princeton University Press.

Nagy, Sharon. 1998. "'This Time I Think I'll Try a Filipina': Global and Local Influences on Relations Between Foreign Household Workers and Their Employers in Doha, Qatar." *City & Society* 10 (no. 1, June): 83–103.

Nascimbene, Bruno. 2008. "The Global Approach to Migration: European Union Policy in the Light of the Implementation of the Hague Programme." *ERA Forum* 9: 291–300.

Newton-Smith, W. H. 1980. *The Structure of Time*. London and Boston: Routledge & Kegan Paul.

Nyers, Peter. 2003. "Abject Cosmopolitanism: The Politics of Protection in the Anti-deportation Movement." *Third World Quarterly* 24 (no. 6): 1069–93.

Oakeshott, Michael. 1995. *Experience and Its Modes*. (First pub. 1933.) Cambridge: Cambridge University Press.

Ong, Aihwa. 1999. *Flexible Citizenship: The Cultural Logics of Transnationality*. Durham, NC: Duke University Press.

———. 2000. "Graduated Sovereignty in South-East Asia." *Theory, Culture and Society* 17: 55–75.

———. 2006. *Neoliberalism as Exception: Mutations in Citizenship and Sovereignty*. Durham, NC: Duke University Press.

Ong, A., and S. Collier, eds. 2005. *Global Assemblages: Technology, Politics, and Ethics as Anthropological Problems*. London: Blackwell.

Ossman, Susan. 1988. "S.O.S. Racisme: Studied Disorder in France." *Socialist Review* 88 (Spring).

———. 1994. *Picturing Casablanca: Portraits of Power in a Modern City*. Berkeley: University of California Press.

———. 1998. "Bob Marley entre nous deux." In *Mimesis: imiter, représenter, circuler*, ed. S. Ossman. Paris: CNRS. (*Hermès,* no. 22.)

———. 2002. *Three Faces of Beauty: Casablanca, Paris, Cairo*. Durham, NC: Duke University Press.

———. 2004. "Studies of Serial Migration." *International Migration* 42 (no. 4, Oct.): 111–21.

———. 2006. "Beck's Cosmopolitan Vision or Plays on the Nation." *Ethnos* 71 (no. 4, Dec.).

———. 2007a. "Introduction." In *The Places We Share: Migration, Subjectivity and Global Mobility*, ed. S. Ossman. Lanham, MD: Lexington Books.

———. 2007b. "Linked Comparisons for Life and Research." In *The Places We Share: Migration, Subjectivity and Global Mobility*, ed. S. Ossman. Lanham, MD: Lexington Books.

———. 2007c. "Cinderella, CV's and Neighborhood *Nemima*: Announcing Morocco's Royal Wedding." *Comparative Studies of South Asia, Africa and the Middle East* 27 (no. 3, Nov./Dec.).

———. 2010. "Making Art Ethnography: Painting, War and Ethnographic Practice." In *Between Art and Anthropology*, ed. A. Schneider and C. Wright. Oxford: Berg.

———. 2011. "First Ladies and Fairytales: Visible Intimacies Remake the Arab World." In *Circuits of Visibility: Gender and Transnational Media Cultures*, ed. R. Hegde and A. Valdivia. New York: New York University Press.

——— and S. Terrio. 2006. "The French Riots: Questioning Spaces of Surveillance and Soverereignty." *International Migration* 44 (no. 2, June): 5–19.

Papademetriou, D. G., D. Meissner, R. Rosenblum, M. Sumtion, et al. 2009. *Aligning Temporary Immigration Visas with US Labor Market Needs: The Case for a New System of Provisional Visas*. Migration Policy Institute, July.

Pellerin, Hélène. 2011. "De la migration à la mobilité: Changement de paradigme dans la gestion migratoire. Le cas du Canada." *Revue européenne des migrations internationales*, 27 (2): 57–75.

Pertierra, Anna Christina. 2007. "Anthropology that Warms your Heart; On Being a Bride in the Field." *Anthropology Matters*, 9, 1.

Peters, John Durham. 1999. *Speaking into the Air: A History of the Idea of Communication*. Chicago: University of Chicago Press.

Rabinow, Paul, and George Marcus, with J. D. Faubion and T. Rees. 2008. *Designs for an Anthropology of the Contemporary.* Durham, NC: Duke University Press.

Rachid, Madawi. 1991. *Politics in an Arabian Oasis.* London: I. B. Tauris.

———, ed. 2005. *Transnational Connections in the Arab Gulf.* London: Routledge.

———. 2009. *Kingdom without Borders: Saudi Arabia's Political, Religious and Media Frontiers.* New York: Columbia/Hurst.

Rattier, Paul-Ernest. 1857. *Paris n'existe pas.* Paris. Self-published.

Regev, Motti. 2007. "Cultural Uniqueness and Aesthetic Cosmopolitanism." *European Journal of Social Theory* 10, 1 (Feb.): 123–38.

Riaño, Yvonne, and Nadia Baghdadi. 2007. "Je pensais que je pourrais avoir une relation plus égalitaire avec un Européen. *Nouvelles Question Féministes,* 26 (no. 1): 38–53.

Ricoeur, Paul. 1984, 1985, 1988. *Time and Narrative (Temps et Récit),* 3 vols., trans. Kathleen McLaughlin and David Pellauer. Chicago: University of Chicago Press.

———. 1990. "Approaches de la personne." In *Lectures 2: La Contrée des philosophes.* Paris: le Seuil.

———. 1992. *Oneself as Another,* trans. Kathleen Blamey. Chicago: University of Chicago Press.

Robbins, Bruce. 1998. "Comparative Cosmopolitanisms." In *Cosmopolitics: Thinking and Feeling Beyond the Nation,* ed. P. Cheah and B. Robbins. Minneapolis: University of Minnesota Press.

Said, Edward. 2000. *Out of Place: A Memoir.* New York. Vintage.

Sassen, Saskia. 2006. *Territory, Authority, Rights, from Medieval Global Assemblages.* Princeton: Princeton University Press.

Sayad, Abdelmalek. 1999. *La Double Absence: Des Illusions de l'Émigré aux Souffrances de l'Émigré.* Paris: le Seuil.

Silverstein, Paul. 2004. *Algeria in France: Transpolitics, Race, and Nation.* Bloomington: Indiana University Press.

Skrbis, Zlatko, and Ian Woodward. 2007. "The Ambivalence of Ordinary Cosmopolitanism: Investigating the Limits of Cosmopolitan Openness." *Sociological Review* 55 (no. 4, Nov.): 730–47.

Smith, William, 2007. "Cosmopolitan Citizenship, Virtue, Irony and Worldliness." *European Journal of Social Theory* 10 (no. 1, Feb.): 37–52.

Steele, Valerie. 1998. *Paris Fashion: A Cultural History.* London: Berg.

Strathern, Marilyn. 2002. "On Space and Depth." In *Complexities: Social Studies of Knowledge Practices*, ed. J. Law and A. Mol. Durham, NC: Duke University Press.

Szerszynski, Bronislaw, and John Urry. 2006. "Visuality, Mobility and the Cosmopolitan: Inhabiting the World from Afar." *British Journal of Sociology* 57 (no. 1): 113–32.

Taussig, Michael. 2011. *I Swear I Saw This: Drawings in Fieldwork Notebooks Namely My Own*. Chicago: University of Chicago Press.

Taylor, Charles. 1989. *Sources of the Self: The Making of the Modern Identity*. Cambridge, MA: Harvard University Press.

Tazi, Nadia. 2007. "Is It Possible to Be Both a Cosmopolitan and a Muslim?" In *Places We Share: Migration, Subjectivity and Global Mobility*, ed. S. Ossman. New York: Lexington.

Terrio, Susan J. 2007. "Zacarias Moussaoui: Moroccan Muslim? French Terrorist? Benighted Zealot? War Criminal? Serial Migrant? All of the Above?" In *Places We Share: Migration, Subjectivity and Global Mobility*, ed. S. Ossman. New York: Lexington.

———. 2009. *Judging Mohammed: Juvenile Delinquency, Immigration, and Exclusion at the Paris Palace of Justice*. Stanford: Stanford University Press.

Thrift, Nigel. 2004. "Movement-Space: The Changing Domain of Thinking Resulting from the Development of New Kinds of Spatial Awareness." *Economy and Society* 33 (no. 4, Nov.): 582–604.

Tuan, Yi-Fu. 1999. *Who Am I? An Autobiography of Emotion, Mind, and Spirit*. Madison: University of Wisconsin Press.

Turner, Brian. 2002. "Cosmopolitan Virtue, Globalization and Patriotism." *Theory, Culture and Society* 19 (nos. 1–2): 45–63.

Turner, Victor. 1974. *Dramas, Fields, and Metaphors: Symbolic Action in Human Society*. Ithaca, NY: Cornell University Press.

———. 1982. *From Ritual to Theater: The Human Seriousness of Play*. New York City: Performing Arts Journal Publications.

Urry, John. 2000. *Sociology Beyond Societies: Mobility for the Twenty-First Century*. London and New York: Routledge.

———. 2007. *Mobilities*. Cambridge: Polity Press.

Van Gennep, Arnold. 1960. *The Rites of Passage*, trans. Monika B. Vizedom and Gabrielle L. Caffe. Chicago: University of Chicago Press.

Venurini, Alessandra. 2008. "Circular Migration as an Employment Strategy for Mediterranean Countries." *CARIM Analytic and Synthetic Notes*, 2008/39, circular Migration Series, Robert Schuman Center for Advanced Studies.

Vertovec, Steven. 2007. "Circular Migration: The Way Forward in Global Policy?" Working papers, International Migration Institute, Oxford University.

Vertovec, Steven, and Robin Cohen. 2002. *Conceiving Cosmopolitanism: Theory, Context and Practice*. Oxford: Oxford University Press.

White, Hayden. 1987. *The Content of the Form: Narrative Discourse and Historical Representation*. Baltimore: Johns Hopkins University Press.

———. 1999. *Figural Realism: Studies in the Mimesis Effect*. Baltimore: Johns Hopkins University Press.

Williams, Bernard. 1993. *Shame and Necessity*. Berkeley: University of California Press.

Wood, Nancy, and Russell King. 2001. *Media and Migration: Constructions of Mobility and Difference*. London: Routledge.

INDEX

DATE DUE
